low-fat no-fat
THAI

low-fat no-fat
THAI

Over 190 delicious and authentic recipes from Thailand, Burma, Indonesia, Malaysia and the Philippines

Jane Bamforth

southwater

This edition is published by Southwater,
an imprint of Anness Publishing Ltd, 108 Great Russell Street,
London WC1B 3NA; info@anness.com

www.southwaterbooks.com; www.annesspublishing.com

If you like the images in this book and would like to investigate using
them for publishing, promotions or advertising, please visit our
website www.practicalpictures.com for more information.

A CIP catalogue record for this book is available from
the British Library.

Publisher: Joanna Lorenz
Editorial Director: Helen Sudell
Editor: Joy Wotton
Recipes: Judy Bastyra, Jane Bamforth, Mridula Baljekar, Jenni
Fleetwood, Yasuko Fukuoka, Christine Ingram, Becky Johnson, Kathy
Man, Sallie Morris, Kate Whiteman
Home Economists: Annabel Ford, Becky Johnson, Lucy McKelvie,
Bridget Sargeson, Helen Trent
Photographers: Martin Brigdale, Nicky Dowey, Janine Hosegood, Becky
Johnson, Dave King, William Lingwood, Craig Robertson
Designer: Nigel Partridge
Production Controller: Ben Worley

NOTES: Bracketed terms are intended for American readers. For all
recipes, quantities are given in both metric and imperial measures
and, where appropriate, in standard cups and spoons.
Follow one set of measures, but not a mixture, because they
are not interchangeable.
Standard spoon and cup measures are level. 1 tsp = 5ml, 1 tbsp =
15ml, 1 cup = 250ml/8fl oz.
Australian standard tablespoons are 20ml. Australian readers should
use 3 tsp in place of 1 tbsp for measuring small quantities.
American pints are 16fl oz/2 cups. American readers should use 20fl
oz/2.5 cups in place of 1 pint when measuring liquids.
Electric oven temperatures in this book are for conventional ovens.
When using a fan oven, the temperature will probably need to be
reduced by about 10–20°C/20–40°F. Since ovens vary, you should
check with your manufacturer's instruction book for guidance.
The nutritional analysis given for each recipe is calculated per portion
(i.e. serving or item), unless otherwise stated. If the recipe gives a
range, such as Serves 4–6, then the nutritional analysis will be for the
smaller portion size, i.e. 6 servings. The analysis does not include
optional ingredients, such as salt added to taste.
Medium (US large) eggs are used unless otherwise stated.
Each recipe title in this book is followed by a symbol that indicates
the following:
★ = 5g of fat or less per serving
★★ = 10g of fat or less per serving
★★★ = 15g of fat or less per serving

Main front cover image shows Stir-fried Baby Squid with Ginger
– for recipe see page 112

CONTENTS

INTRODUCTION   6

THE LOW-FAT THAI AND
SOUTH-EAST ASIAN KITCHEN   8

    HEALTHY EATING GUIDELINES   10
    PLANNING A LOW-FAT DIET   12
    FAT-FREE COOKING METHODS   13
    VEGETABLES   14
    FRUIT, NUTS AND SEEDS   16
    HERBS AND SPICES   17
    RICE   18
    NOODLES AND WRAPPERS   20
    TOFU AND SOYA PRODUCTS   22
    MEAT AND POULTRY   23
    FISH AND SHELLFISH   24
    FAT AND CALORIE
      CONTENTS OF FOOD   26

SOUPS   28

APPETIZERS AND LIGHT BITES   56

VEGETARIAN MAIN DISHES   82

FISH AND SHELLFISH   100

CHICKEN AND DUCK   128

MEAT DISHES   150

RICE AND NOODLES   176

VEGETABLES AND SALADS   198

DESSERTS   228

GLOSSARY   250

MAP   251

INDEX   252

THE LOW-FAT THAI AND SOUTH-EAST ASIAN KITCHEN

Cooks in Thailand and South-east Asia have much to teach us

about low-fat cooking. Their traditional diet is largely

composed of vegetables, with a healthy proportion of

carbohydrate in the form of noodles or rice, protein in the form

of tofu or only small amounts of meat or fish. Suggestions for

using tofu and other ingredients typical of the region are given

in this section, which also includes valuable advice about

planning and maintaining a healthy low-fat diet.

HEALTHY EATING GUIDELINES

A healthy diet provides us with all the nutrients we need. By eating the right types, balance and proportions of foods, we are more likely to have more energy and a higher resistance to diseases and illnesses such as heart disease, cancers, bowel disorders and obesity.

By choosing a variety of foods every day, you are supplying your body with all the essential nutrients it needs. To get the balance right, it is important to know just how much of each type of food you should be eating.

Of the five main food groups, it is recommended that we eat at least five portions of fruit and vegetables a day, not including potatoes; carbohydrate foods such as noodles, cereals, rice and potatoes; moderate amounts of fish, poultry and dairy products; and small amounts of foods containing fat or sugar. A dish like Thai Fried Rice fits the prescription perfectly, with its balance of rice, chicken fillets, (bell) peppers and corn.

THE ROLE OF FAT IN THE DIET

Fats shouldn't be cut out of our diets completely, as they are a valuable source of energy and make foods more palatable. However, lowering the fats, especially saturated fats, in your diet, may help you to lose weight, as well as reducing your risk of developing diseases.

Aim to limit your daily intake of fats to no more than 30–35 per cent of the total number of calories you consume. Each gram of fat provides nine calories, so a person eating 2,000 calories a day should not eat more than 70g/2¾oz of fat. Saturated fat should not comprise more than 10 per cent of the total calorie intake.

TYPES OF FAT

All fats in our foods are made up of building blocks of fatty acids and glycerol, and their properties vary according to each combination.

The two main types of fat are saturated and unsaturated. The unsaturated group is divided into

two further categories – polyunsaturated and monounsaturated fats. There is usually a combination of these types of unsaturated fat in foods that contain fat, but the amount of each type varies from one kind of food to another.

SATURATED FATS

These fats are usually hard at room temperature. They are not essential in the diet, and should be limited, as they are implicated in raising the level of cholesterol in the blood, which can increase the likelihood of heart disease.

The main sources of saturated fats are animal products, such as fatty cuts of meat and meat products; spreading fats that are solid at room temperature, such as butter, lard and margarine; and

Below: Thai and South-east Asian cooking makes use of a wide variety of herbs, spices and flavourings, including cinnamon, root ginger, garlic, lemon grass and kaffir limes.

Above: Asian cooks have a wonderful assortment of shellfish, such as mussels, from the sea, lakes, rivers and canals.

Above: Rice noodles and rice vermicelli form an integral part of the Thai and South-east Asian cuisine. Easily reconstituted, they are virtually fat free.

Above: Naturally low in fat, such fresh green vegetables as these snake or yard-long beans form a healthy part of the Thai diet.

full-fat dairy products such as cream and cheese. Aside from meat, these ingredients are seldom found in Thai and South-east Asian recipes, but it is also important to avoid coconut and palm oil, which are saturated fats of vegetable origin. More insidious are those fats which, when processed, change the nature of the fat from unsaturated fatty acids to saturated ones. These are called "hydrogenated" fats, and should be strictly limited, so look out for that term on food labels.

Saturated fats are also found in many processed foods, such as chips (French fries) and savoury snacks, as well as cookies, pastries and cakes.

POLYUNSATURATED FATS

Small amounts of polyunsaturated fats are essential for good health, as they provide energy, can help to reduce cholesterol levels and enable the absorption of the fat-soluble vitamins A and D. The body can't manufacture polyunsaturated fatty acids, so they must be obtained from food. There are two types: those of vegetable or plant origin, known as Omega-6, which are found in sunflower oil, soft margarine, nuts and seeds; and Omega-3 fatty acids, which come from oily fish such

as tuna, salmon, herring, mackerel and sardines as well as walnuts, soya beans, wheatgerm and rapeseed (canola) oil.

MONOUNSATURATED FATS

The best known monounsaturated fat is olive oil. This is not used in Asian cooking, but another monounsaturated oil, groundnut (peanut) oil, is a popular choice. It is ideal for stir-frying and gives food a delicious flavour. Monounsaturated fatty acids are also found in nuts such as almonds, and oily fish. They are thought to have the beneficial effect of reducing blood cholesterol levels.

THE CHOLESTEROL QUESTION

Cholesterol is a fat-like substance that occurs naturally in the body, and which we also acquire from food. It has a vital role, since it is the material from which many essential hormones and vitamin D are made. Cholesterol is carried around the body, attached to proteins called high density lipoproteins (HDLs), low density lipoproteins (LDLs) and very low density lipoproteins (VLDLs or triglycerides).

Eating too much saturated fat encourages the body to make more cholesterol than it can use or can rid itself of. After food has been consumed, the LDLs carry the fat in the blood to

the cells where it is required. Any surplus should be excreted from the body, but if there are too many LDLs in the blood, some of the fat will be deposited on the walls of the arteries. This furring up gradually narrows the arteries and is one of the most common causes of heart attacks and strokes.

By way of contrast, HDLs appear to protect against heart disease. Whether high triglyceride levels are risk factors remains unknown.

CUTTING DOWN ON FATS AND SATURATED FATS IN THE DIET

It is relatively easy to cut down on obvious sources of fat in the diet, like butter, oils, margarine, cream, whole milk and full-fat cheese, but it is also important to know about and check consumption of "hidden" fats.

By educating yourself and being aware of which foods are high in fats, and by making simple changes, you can reduce the total fat content of your diet quite considerably. Choose low-fat alternatives when selecting items like coconut milk, milk, cheese and salad dressings. Fill up with very low-fat foods, such as fruits and vegetables, and foods that are high in carbohydrates, such as bread, potatoes, rice or noodles.

PLANNING A LOW-FAT DIET

Cutting down on fat on an everyday basis means we need to keep a close eye on the fat content of everything we eat. These general guidelines on reducing fat are applicable to all cuisines.

CUTTING DOWN ON FAT IN THE DIET

Most of us eat far more fat than we require – consuming about 115g/4oz of fat every day. Yet just 10g/¼oz, the amount in a single packet of crisps (US potato chips) or a thin slice of Cheddar cheese, is all that we actually need.

Current nutritional thinking is more lenient than this and suggests an upper daily limit of about 70g/2¾oz total fat.

Using low-fat recipes helps to reduce the overall daily intake of fat, but there are also lots of other ways of reducing the fat in your diet. Just follow the "eat less, try instead" suggestions below to discover how easy it can be.

• Eat less butter, margarine, other spreading fats and cooking oils. Try reduced-fat spreads, low-fat spreads or fat-free spreads. Butter or hard margarine should be softened at room temperature so that they can be spread thinly. Try low-fat cream cheese or low-fat soft cheese for sandwiches and toast.

Above: For fat-free snacks that are always available, keep an exotic supply of fresh fruit to hand including star fruit (carambola), papaya and lychees.

• Eat less full-fat dairy products such as whole milk, cream, butter, hard margarine, crème fraîche, whole-milk yogurts and hard cheese. Try instead semi-skimmed (low-fat) or skimmed milk, low-fat or reduced-fat milk products, such as low-fat yogurts and soft cheeses, reduced-fat hard cheeses such as Cheddar, and reduced-fat crème fraîche.

• Silken tofu can be used instead of cream in soups and sauces. It is a good source of calcium and an excellent protein food.

• Eat fewer fatty cuts of meat and high-fat meat products, such as pâtés, burgers, pies and sausages. Try instead naturally low-fat meats such as skinless chicken and turkey, ostrich and venison. When cooking lamb, beef or pork, use only the leanest cuts. Always cut away any visible fat and skin from meat before cooking. Try substituting low-fat protein ingredients like dried beans, lentils or tofu for some or all of the meat in a recipe.

• Eat more fish. It is easy to cook, tastes great, and if you use a steamer, you won't need to add any extra fat at all.

• Eat fewer hard cooking fats, such as lard or hard margarine. Try instead polyunsaturated or monounsaturated oils, such as sunflower or corn oil, and don't use too much.

• Eat fewer rich salad dressings and less full-fat mayonnaise. Try reduced-fat or fat-free dressings, or just a squeeze of lemon juice. Use a reduced-fat mayonnaise and thin it with puréed silken tofu for an even greater fat saving.

• Eat less fried food. Try fat-free cooking methods like steaming, grilling (broiling), baking or microwaving. Use non-stick pans with spray oil. When roasting or grilling meat, place it on a rack and drain off excess fat frequently.

• Eat fewer deep-fried or sautéed potatoes. Boil or bake them instead, or use other carbohydrates. Avoid chow-mein noodles, which are high in fat.

Above: Tuna and salmon are good sources of Omega-3 fatty acids, phytochemicals and antioxidants, which work together for a healthy heart.

• Cut down on oil when cooking. Drain fried food on kitchen paper to remove as much oil as possible. Choose heavy, good-quality non-stick pans and use spray oil for the lightest coverage. Moisten food with fat-free or low-fat liquids such as fruit juice, defatted stock, wine or even beer.

• Eat fewer high-fat snacks, such as chocolate, cookies, chips (French fries) and crisps. Try instead a piece of fruit, some vegetable crudités or some home-baked low-fat fruit cake.

Below: Choose lean cuts of meat and naturally low-fat meats such as skinless chicken and turkey.

FAT-FREE COOKING METHODS

Thai and South-east Asian cooking uses a variety of low-fat and fat-free cooking methods, and by incorporating recipes from this region into your daily diet it is easy to bring down your total fat consumption. Where possible, steam, microwave or grill (broil) foods, without adding extra fat. Alternatively, braise in a defatted stock, wine or fruit juice, or stir-fry with just a spray of vegetable oil.

• By choosing a good quality, non-stick wok, such as the one above, you can keep the amount of fat needed for cooking foods to the absolute minimum. When cooking meat in a regular pan, dry-fry the meat to brown it, then tip it into a sieve (strainer) and drain off the excess fat before returning it to the pan and adding the other ingredients. If you do need a little fat for cooking, choose an oil high in unsaturates, such as sunflower or corn oil and use a spray where possible.

• Eat less meat and more vegetables and noodles or other forms of pasta. A good method for making a small amount of meat such as beef steak go a long way is to place it in the freezer for 30 minutes and then slice it very thinly with a sharp knife. Meat prepared this way will cook very quickly with very little fat.

• When baking chicken or fish, wrap it in a loose package of foil or baking parchment, with a little wine or fruit juice. Add some fresh herbs or spices before sealing the parcel, if you like.

• It is often unnecessary to add fat when grilling (broiling) food. If the food shows signs of drying, lightly brush or spray it with a little unsaturated oil, such as sunflower, corn or olive oil. Microwaved foods seldom need the addition of fat, so add herbs or spices for extra flavour and colour.

• Steaming is the ideal way of cooking fish. If you like, arrange the fish on a bed of aromatic flavourings such as lemon or lime slices and sprigs of herbs. Alternatively, place finely shredded vegetables or seaweed in the base of the steamer to give the fish extra flavour.

• If you do not own a steamer, cook vegetables in a covered pan over low heat with just a little water, so that they cook in their own juices.
• Vegetables can be braised in the oven in low-fat or fat-free stock, wine or a little water with some chopped fresh or dried herbs.
• Try poaching foods such as chicken, fish or fruit in low-fat or fat-free stock or fruit juice.
• Plain rice or noodles make a very good low-fat accompaniment to most Thai and South-east Asian dishes.

• The classic Asian technique of adding moisture and flavour to chicken by marinating it in a mixture of soy sauce and rice wine, with a little sesame oil, can be used with other meats too. You can also use a mixture of alcohol, herbs and spices, or vinegar or fruit juice. The marinade will also help to tenderize the meat and any remaining marinade can be used to baste the food while it is cooking.
• When serving vegetables, resist the temptation to add butter. Instead, sprinkle with chopped fresh herbs.

Low-fat spreads in cooking
A huge variety of low-fat and reduced-fat spreads is available in supermarkets, along with some spreads that are very low in fat. Generally speaking, any very low-fat spreads with a fat content of around 20 per cent or less have a high water content. These are unsuitable for cooking and can only be used for spreading.

VEGETABLES

Naturally low in fat and bursting with vitamins and minerals, vegetables are one food group that should ideally make up the bulk of our daily diet. In Thailand and South-east Asia cooks use vegetables freely in stir-fries and braised dishes, and have evolved a wide range of delicious vegetarian main courses to make the most of the abundant choice of vegetables on sale in markets.

Many of these vegetables are now commonplace in other parts of the world. Chinese leaves (Chinese cabbage), pak choi (bok choy) and beansprouts are usually available in supermarkets, and other greens, such as mizuna, Chinese mustard greens and Chinese broccoli, are often grown by small producers and can be found at farmers' markets.

CHINESE LEAVES

Also known as Chinese cabbage or Napa cabbage, this vegetable has pale green, crinkly leaves with long, wide, white ribs. It is pleasantly crunchy, has a sweet, nutty flavour and tastes wonderful raw or cooked. When buying Chinese leaves, look out for firm, slightly heavy heads with pale green leaves without blemishes or bruises. To prepare, peel off the outer leaves, cut off the root and slice the cabbage thinly or thickly. When stir-fried, Chinese leaves lose their subtle cabbage taste and take on the flavour of other ingredients in the dish.

Below: Chinese leaves have a mild, delicate flavour.

Right: Pak choi tastes similar to spinach.

PAK CHOI

Another member of the brassica family, pak choi (bok choy) has lots of noms-de-plume, including horse's ear, Chinese cabbage and Chinese white cabbage. There are several varieties, and one or other is usually on sale at the supermarket. Unlike Chinese leaves, pak choi doesn't keep well, so plan to use it within a day or two of purchase. The vegetable is generally cooked, although very young and tender pak choi can be eaten raw. The stems – regarded by many as the best part – need slightly longer cooking than the leaves.

CHOI SUM

Often sold in bunches, choi sum is a brassica with bright green leaves and thin, pale, slightly grooved stems. It has a pleasant aroma and mild taste, and remains crisp and tender if properly cooked. The leaves can be sliced, but are more often steamed whole. Choi sum will keep for a few days in the salad drawer, but is best used as soon as possible after purchase.

CHINESE BROCCOLI

With its somewhat straggly appearance, this brassica looks more like purple sprouting broccoli than prim Calabrese. Every part of Chinese broccoli is edible, and each has its own inimitable taste. To prepare, remove the tough outer leaves, then cut off the leaves. If the stems are tough, peel them. It is usual to blanch the vegetable briefly in salted boiling water or stock before stir-frying.

AUBERGINES

Popular throughout Thailand and South-east Asia, aubergines (eggplants) come in a variety of shapes, sizes and colours. They have a smoky, slightly bitter taste and spongy flesh that readily absorbs other flavours and oils. To avoid the absorption of too much fat, cut the aubergine into slices, and dry-fry these in a wok over medium heat for 4–5 minutes. They can also be braised, stuffed or baked.

MOOLI

Also known as daikon, this Asian vegetable looks rather like a parsnip, but is actually related to the radish. The flavour is milder than that of most radishes, however, although the texture is similar: crisp and crunchy. Treat it like a carrot, scraping or peeling the outer skin and then slicing it in rounds or batons. It can be eaten raw or cooked.

BAMBOO SHOOTS

Fresh bamboo shoots are quite hard to buy outside Asia, but you may find them in big-city Asian markets. They must be parboiled before being cooked, as the raw vegetable contains a highly toxic oil. Remove the base and the hard outer leaves, then cut the core into chunks. Boil these in salted water for 30 minutes, then drain, rinse under cold water and drain again. Cut into slices, shreds or cubes for further cooking. Dried bamboo slices must be soaked in water for 2–3 hours before use. Canned bamboo shoots only need rinsing before being used.

Below: Choi sum is often used in stir-fries.

Above: Thai cooking uses green apple aubergines and purple long aubergines.

WATER CHESTNUTS

Fresh, crisp water chestnuts are the corms of a plant that grows on the margins of rivers and lakes. Their snow-white flesh stays crunchy even after long cooking. Fresh water chestnuts are often available from Asian markets. They keep well in a paper bag in the refrigerator. Once released from their dark brown jackets, they must be kept submerged in water in a covered container and used within one week. Canned water chestnuts should be rinsed before being used.

Below: Mooli has a crisp, crunchy texture and is delicious raw.

BEANSPROUTS

Mung beans and soy beans are the varieties of beansprout most often used, and they are an important ingredient in the Asian kitchen. It is important to use them as fresh as possible. Better still, sprout the beans yourself. Before use, rinse them to remove the husks and tiny roots. Use them in salads or stir-fries, but take care not to overcook them, or they will become limp and tasteless.

SPRING ONIONS

Slender and crisp, spring onions (scallions) are appreciated by Asian cooks not only for their aroma and flavour, but also for their perceived cooling qualities. Use spring onions raw in salads or lightly cooked in stir-fries. They need very little preparation. Just trim off the roots, strip off the wilted outer leaves and separate the white and green parts. Spring onion green is sometimes used in Asian dishes as ribbon, to tie tiny parcels of food, in which case it is first blanched so that it becomes more flexible.

MUSHROOMS

Several types of mushrooms are used in Asian cooking, and many of these are now available in Western supermarkets.

Shiitake mushrooms are prized in Asia, both for their flavour and their medicinal qualities. They have a slightly acidic taste and a meaty, slippery texture. They contain twice as much protein as button mushrooms and their robust flavour makes them the ideal partner for noodles and rice.

To prepare fresh shiitake mushrooms, remove the stems. The caps can be left whole, or sliced. If they are to be used in a salad, cook them briefly in low-fat stock first.

Dried shiitake mushrooms must be reconstituted before being used. Soak them in cold water overnight, or in a bowl of warm water for at least 30 minutes before using, then strain the soaking liquid. Remove the stems before use.

Right: Spring onions are used raw in salads.

Oyster mushrooms have a mild flavour and are pastel-coloured in shades of pink, yellow or pearl grey. They need gentle handling. Tear, rather than cut, large specimens and don't overcook them, or they will become rubbery.

Enokitake mushrooms are tiny, with bud-like caps at the end of long, slender stems. To appreciate their crisp texture and sweet flavour, use them raw in salads.

SHALLOTS

Although they belong to the same family as garlic, leeks, chives and onions – and look suspiciously like baby onions – shallots are very much their own vegetable. Sometimes called bunching onions, they have bulbs that multiply to produce clusters joined at the root end.

Shallots tend to be sweeter and much milder than large onions. Some Thai varieties are sweet enough to be used in desserts.

Indispensable in South-east Asian kitchens, shallots are far more popular than both regular onions and spring onions (scallions) for everyday use. Ground with garlic, ginger and other aromatics, shallots form the standard marinade and are also an essential ingredient in curry pastes and satay sauce. Dried shallots (hanh huong) are a popular alternative in Vietnam.

Preparation and cooking techniques: Trim the shallots, peel off the skin, then prise the bulbs apart. Leave these whole for braising, or chop as required. Thinly-sliced shallot rings are sometimes dry-fried until crisp, then used as a garnish.

Shallots will keep for several months in a cool, dry place.

FRUIT, NUTS AND SEEDS

When embarking on a low-fat eating plan, it is all too easy to concentrate solely on the fat content of foods while ignoring the amount of sugar they contain. Avoid following a sensible main course with a sugary dessert. Instead, end a meal with a piece of fresh fruit or a few nuts. The latter can be high in fat, but, with the exception of brazil nuts and coconuts, the fat in nuts is monounsaturated or polyunsaturated, and cholesterol-free.

LYCHEES

These moist fruits need no preparation once you have cracked the shells and peeled off the scaly red skin. The pearly white flesh inside can be sliced and used in a fruit salad or savoury dish. South-east Asian cooks like to pair lychees with pork. For a delectable sorbet, try puréed lychees with elderflower syrup. When buying fresh lychees, choose ones with pink or red shells; brown fruit are past their prime.

PINEAPPLES

The raw fruit and juice are very popular in Thailand, but pineapple is also used in cooked sweet and savoury dishes. Fresh pineapple will keep in a cool place for up to a week. To prepare pineapple, cut off the leaves, then quarter lengthways or cut in slices. Remove the skin and "eyes".

MANGOES

Most mangoes are oval in shape with blushed gold or pink skin. The easiest way to obtain mango chunks is to cut a thick lengthways slice off each side of the unpeeled fruit. Score the flesh on each slice with criss-cross lines. Fold these slices inside out and slice off the flesh.

PAPAYAS

Papayas or paw-paws can be small and round, but are usually pear-shaped. When ripe, the flesh is eaten as it is or used in fruit salads and other desserts. Papayas that are not too ripe can be added to soups, curries or seafood dishes. Unripe green papayas are served raw in salads and made into pickles. The juice and skins are used to tenderize meat.

LIME

These small, green and very sour citrus fruits are used extensively throughout the region. Fresh lime juice is served as a drink, with salt and sugar, and is also used in salad dressings.

COCONUT MILK AND CREAM

Coconut milk is high in fat but there is a version that is 88 per cent fat free. Coconut milk and cream are both made from the grated flesh of the coconut, and in the East, one can buy bags of freshly grated coconut for just this purpose. Warm water is added and the coconut is squeezed until the mixture is cloudy. When strained, this is coconut milk. If the milk is left to stand, coconut cream will float to the surface.

Left: Canned and fresh lychees have a wonderful scented aroma.

STAR FRUIT

The correct name for this fruit is carambola. Cylindrical in shape, the bright yellow waxy-looking fruit has five distinctive "wings" or protuberances which form the points of the star shapes revealed when the fruit is sliced. The flavour varies: fruits picked straight from the tree in Asia are inevitably sweet and scented, but those that have travelled long distances in cold storage can be disappointing.

PEANUTS

One of the most important flavourings in Thai cooking, peanuts are not especially low in fat but a small amount can make all the difference to the character of a dish. Raw peanuts have little smell, but once cooked they have a powerful aroma, a crunchy texture and a distinctive flavour. Peanuts play an important role in Asian cuisine. The smaller ones are used for making oil, while the larger, less oily nuts are widely eaten, both as a snack food and as ingredients in salads and main courses.

SESAME SEEDS

These tiny seeds are flat and pear-shaped. Raw sesame seeds have very little aroma and they are almost tasteless until they are roasted or dry-fried, which brings out their distinctive nutty flavour and aroma.

LOTUS SEEDS

Fresh lotus seeds are used as a snack food. The dried seeds must be soaked in water before use. The seeds are prized for their texture and ability to absorb other flavours. They are often added to soups.

HERBS AND SPICES

The principal flavourings favoured in South-east Asia have made a tremendous contribution to global cuisine. Ingredients like fresh ginger, lemon grass and kaffir lime now feature on menus the world over, not just in recipes that reflect their origin, but also in fusion food. Fish sauce is an essential seasoning for Thai and Vietnamese cooking, in much the same way that soy sauce is important to the Chinese and Japanese.

GARLIC

Often used with spring onions (scallions) and ginger, garlic is a vital ingredient in Thai and South-east Asian dishes. The most common variety has a purple skin, a fairly distinctive aroma and a hint of sweetness. Garlic may dominate a dish, but it may also impart a mild flavour, as when a garlic clove is heated in oil and then removed from the pan.

GALANGAL

Galangal is slightly harder than ginger, but used in much the same way. When young, the skin is creamy white with pink sprouts and the flavour is lemony. As galangal matures, the flavour intensifies and becomes more peppery.

GINGER

Valued not just as an aromatic, but also for its medicinal qualities, ginger is used throughout Asia. When young, ginger is juicy and tender, with a sharp flavour suggestive of citrus. At this stage it can easily be sliced, chopped or pounded to a paste. Older roots are tougher and may need to be peeled and grated. Pickled ginger is delicious. It can be served as a side dish, or combined with other ingredients such as beef or duck.

CHILLIES

Although they did not originate in South-east Asia, chillies have been embraced so fervently by Thailand that they are now irrevocably associated with the area. They are an essential ingredient in a variety of South-east Asian cuisines. But it is for their flavour rather than their fire that they are most valued. Be careful when you handle chillies. They contain a substance called capsaicin, which is a powerful irritant. If this comes into contact with delicate skin or the eyes, it can cause considerable pain. Wear gloves when handling chillies or wash your hands thoroughly in hot soapy water afterwards.

LEMON GRASS

A perennial tufted plant with a bulbous base, lemon grass looks like a plump spring onion (scallion). When the stalk is cut or bruised, the lively citrus aroma becomes evident. There are two main ways of using lemon grass. The stalk can be kept whole, bruised, then cooked slowly in liquid until it releases its flavour and is removed, or the tender lower portion of the stalk can be sliced or finely chopped and then stir-fried.

KAFFIR LIME LEAVES

These fruit are not true limes, but belong to a subspecies of the citrus family. Native to South-east Asia, they have green knobbly skins. The fruit is not edible, but the rind is sometimes used

Left: Red and green chillies

in cooking, but it is the leaves that are most highly prized. Kaffir lime leaves are synonymous with Thai cooking. The leaves are torn or finely shredded and used in soups and curries. Finely grated rind is added to fish or chicken dishes.

BASIL

Three types of basil are grown in Thailand, each with a slightly different appearance, flavour and use. Thai basil has a sweet, anise flavour and is used in red curries. Holy basil is pungent and tastes like cloves. Lemon basil is used in soups and is sprinkled on salads.

CORIANDER/CILANTRO

The entire coriander plant is used in Thai cooking – roots, stems, leaves and seeds. The fresh, delicate leaves are used in sauces, curries and for garnishes. The roots and stems are crushed and used for marinades. The seeds are ground to add flavour to various curry pastes.

*Above:
Lemon grass*

FISH SAUCE

Thai *nam pla* or fish sauce has a slightly stronger flavour and aroma than the Vietnamese or Chinese versions. It is used in Asia as a seasoning in all kinds of savoury dishes. It is also blended with extra flavourings such as finely chopped garlic and chillies, and sugar and lime juice to make a dipping sauce.

CURRY PASTES

Most Thai curries are based on "wet" spice mixtures, made by grinding spices and aromatics in a heavy mortar with a rough surface. Red curry paste is used in beef dishes and robust chicken dishes. Green curry paste, made from herbs and fresh green chillies, is used for chicken curries. Yellow curry paste and, the mildest of all, Mussaman curry paste are used for chicken and beef curries.

RICE

This low-fat high carbohydrate food is immensely important in Thai and South-east Asian cooking. When Thais are called to the table, the phrase used – *gkin kao* – literally translates as "a time to eat rice". All the other foods that make up a meal – meat, fish and vegetables – are regarded as accompaniments and are referred to as *ghap kao* or "things eaten with rice".

Rice is a non-allergenic food, rich in complex carbohydrates and low in salts and fats. It contains small amounts of easily digestible protein, together with phosphorous, magnesium, potassium and zinc. Brown rice, which retains the bran, yields vitamin E and some B-group vitamins, and is also a source of fibre. Although it is healthier than white rice, it is the latter that is preferred in South-east Asia.

The average Thai eats 158kg/350lb of rice every year, which is almost a pound a day. It is consumed in various forms, from basic steamed rice to rice noodles, crackers and cakes.

Two distinct types of rice are popular in Thailand. The first is a delicately scented long grain variety, which is used as a staple with all meals. It comes in several qualities, and is white and fluffy with separate grains when cooked. In northern Thailand, a starchy glutinous rice is preferred. When cooked, the grains stick together.

There are thousands of varieties of rice, many of which are known only in the areas where they are cultivated. The simplest method of classification is by the length of the grain, which can be long, medium or short. Long grain rice is three or four times as long as it is wide.

Rice Mother
The traditional rice-growing communities in Thailand have a high regard for *Mae Pra Posop*, the "Rice Mother". Elaborate ceremonies are performed in her name during various stages of rice cultivation so that she may bless the fields with bountiful harvests from year to year.

Above: Jasmine or Thai fragrant rice has tender, aromatic grains and is popular throughout central and southern Thailand and much of South-east Asia. It is widely available in supermarkets and Asian stores in the West.

JASMINE RICE

Also known as fragrant or scented rice, this long grain variety is the staple food of the central and southern parts of Thailand. As the name suggests, jasmine rice has a delicate aroma. The flavour is slightly nutty, and it resembles Basmati rice from India. The uncooked grains are translucent and, when cooked, the rice is fluffy and white. Most of the crop comes from a region between central and north-eastern Thailand where the soil is a combination of clay and sand. Newly harvested rice from this region is prized for the delicate texture of the grains.

GLUTINOUS RICE

Commonly referred to as sweet or sticky rice, glutinous rice is the mainstay of the diet in the northern and north-eastern regions of Thailand. It is delicious and very filling. The name is derived entirely from its sticky texture, as rice does not contain any gluten. Easily cultivated on the hillsides and high plateaux of these regions, glutinous rice requires less water during the growing period than the wet rice of the central lowlands.

Glutinous rice comes in both short or round grain and long grain varieties. Thai people prefer the long grain

Below: Glutinous rice, which may be black (although, more accurately, it is a very dark red), white or a hybrid known as "jasmine sweet", is most widely used in north and north-east Thailand.

Above: Rice is best cooked using the absorption method. Cook the rice with water in a tightly covered pan, then leave for 5 minutes until tender before serving.

variety; the short grain rice is more commonly used in Japanese and Chinese cooking. Some of the long grain varieties have a delicate, aromatic flavour, and these high-grade hybrids are sometimes labelled "jasmine sweet" or "jasmine glutinous rice", the adjective "jasmine" echoing the description used for their fragrant cousins in the non-glutinous rice family.

What makes this type of rice unusual is the way in which the grains clump together when cooked, enabling it to be eaten with the hands. Bitesize chunks of cooked rice are pulled off, one at a time, and rolled to a ball between the fingers and palm of the right hand. The ball is then dunked in a sauce or stew before being eaten. The process is not as messy as it sounds; if it is done correctly, then the grains stick to each other but not to the fingers or the palm. At the end of a meal, rolling the last piece of rice can actually have a cleansing effect, as the rice mops up any remaining juices or grease on the hand.

The starchiness of glutinous rice gives the uncooked grain a distinct opaque white colour, which is different from the more translucent appearance

of regular rice grains. When soaked and steamed, however, the reverse is true. Glutinous rice becomes translucent, while regular rice turns opaque.

Although it is in the north and the north-eastern regions of Thailand that glutinous rice is most popular, it is also eaten elsewhere in the country, most frequently in sweet snacks or desserts. The rice is sweetened and flavoured with coconut milk, and is especially popular in the mango and durian season, when huge amounts of the coconut-flavoured rice are sold to eat with these precious fruits. Use low-fat coconut milk to keep the fat content as low as possible.

BLACK GLUTINOUS RICE

This wholegrain rice – that is, with only the husk removed – has a rich, nutty flavour that is distinctly different from the more subtle taste of white glutinous rice. It is generally sweetened with coconut milk and sugar and eaten as a snack or dessert, rather than being used as the staple of a savoury meal. Reduced-fat coconut milk makes an excellent substitute. It does tend to be quite heavy, filling and indigestible if eaten in quantity, so it is usually nibbled as a sweetmeat snack in the mid-afternoon or later in the evening, after the evening meal has been digested. A popular version of roasted glutinous rice, flattened into a cake, is *khao mow rang*, which is sold at all markets throughout Thailand.

In spite of its name, black rice isn't actually black in colour. If the grains are soaked in water for a few hours, the water will turn a deep burgundy red, showing the rice's true colour.

RICE PRODUCTS

Throughout Thailand and South-east Asia, rice, the staple carbohydrate, is used in many different ways.

Rice Flour

This flour may be made from either glutinous or non-glutinous raw rice that has been very finely ground. It is used to make the dough for fresh rice noodles and is also used to make

Above: Rice flour is finely ground and thoroughly pulverized. As a result, it has a very light texture and is used for fresh rice noodles.

desserts such as pancakes. Rice flour is readily available in Asian food stores. When the source is non-glutinous rice it is called *paeng khao jao* and when it is made from glutinous rice it is known as *paeng khao niao*. Store it as you would wheat flour.

Fermented Rice

Made by fermenting cooked glutinous rice, this is a popular sweetmeat, sold on market stalls and by street vendors.

Rice-pot Crust

In several cultures, the crust that forms on the base of the pan when rice is cooked in a particular way is highly prized. In Thailand, the crust is lifted off the base of the pan in sheets and is then dried out in the sun before being sold. *Khao tang* is lightly toasted or fried before being eaten.

To make *khao tang* at home, spread a layer of cooked rice about 5mm/¼in thick on a lightly greased baking sheet. Dry it out in a low oven, 140°C/275°F/Gas 1, for several hours. Leave to cool, then break into pieces. Deep-fry for just a few seconds until puffed, but not browned. Lift out using a slotted spoon and drain on kitchen paper.

NOODLES AND WRAPPERS

Second only to rice in importance in the Thai diet, noodles and wrappers are cooked in a vast number of ways. Noodles are eaten at any time of day, including breakfast, and if hunger strikes unexpectedly, one of the many roadside noodle carts will furnish a tasty snack. For the local population, soup noodles are easily the most popular dish, but tourists tend to plump for *Pad Thai* (fried noodles). Wrappers are wrapped around all kinds of fillings.

NOODLES

There are basically five main varieties of noodles used in Thai cooking: *sen ya*, *ba mee*, *sen mee*, *sen lek* and *wun sen*. Most can be bought fresh in Asian stores, but it is more likely that you will find them dried. Noodles come in several sizes, from tiny transparent threads to large sheets. Many of them are made from rice, which serves to further emphasize the importance of the grain in the Thai diet. Other types of noodles are based on wheat flour or flour made from ground mung beans.

Unfortunately, the names of noodles are not standardized and the same type of noodle may go under several different names, depending on the manufacturer or which part of the country they come from. Noodles made without eggs are often labelled "imitation noodles" or "alimentary paste".

Noodle know-how

Both dried and fresh noodles have to be cooked in boiling water before use – or soaked in boiling water until pliable. How long for depends on the type of noodle, their thickness and whether or not the noodles are going to be cooked again in a soup or sauce. As a rule, once they have been soaked, dried noodles require about 3 minutes' cooking, while fresh ones will often be ready in less than a minute and may need to be rinsed under cold water to prevent them from overcooking.

Below: Dried vermicelli rice noodles should be soaked, not boiled.

RICE NOODLES

Both fresh and dried rice noodles are available in Thai markets. Fresh noodles are highly perishable, and they must be cooked as soon as possible after purchase. Rice noodles are available in a wide range of shapes and widths from fine vermicelli to thick, round rice noodle nests.

Vermicelli Rice Noodles

These noodles are usually sold dried and must be soaked in boiling water before use. When dried, rice vermicelli are known as rice stick noodles.

Medium Rice Noodles

Resembling spaghetti, these noodles are usually sold dried. The city of Chanthaburi in Thailand is famous for *sen lek* noodles, which are sometimes called *Jantoboon* noodles after the nickname for the town.

Rice Stick Noodles

Also known as rice river noodles, these noodles are sold both dried and fresh, although the latter form is more popular. When fresh rice stick noodles tend to be rather sticky and need to be separated before being cooked.

Rice Noodle Nests

Although the Thai name of these fresh thick round rice noodles means Chinese noodles, these are actually a Thai speciality, made of rice flour. In the Lacquer Pavilion of Suan Pakkad Palace there is a panel showing the making of *khanom chine* as part of the preparations for the Buddha's last meal.

Khanom chine are white and the strands are a little thicker than spaghetti. At most markets in Thailand, nests of these noodles are a familiar sight. They are sold freshly cooked. You buy them by the hundred nests and should allow four or five nests per person. Buy the cheaper ones, because they taste better although they are not so white as the more expensive noodle nests. Fresh noodles are highly perishable, so, even though they are cooked, it makes sense to buy them early in the day, and steam them again when you get them home.

Fresh noodles are delicious when served with *nam ya*, *nam prik*, *sow nam* and a variety of curries.

Below: Rice stick noodles are flat, not unlike Italian tagliatelle.

Preparing rice noodles is a simple matter. They need only to be soaked in hot water for a few minutes to soften them before serving. Add the noodles to a large bowl of just-boiled water and leave for 5–10 minutes, or until they soften, stirring occasionally to separate the strands. Their dry weight will usually double after soaking, so 115g/4oz dry noodles will produce about 225g/8oz after soaking.

Rice stick noodles puff up and become wonderfully crisp when they are deep-fried. Just a few deep-fried noodles sprinkled over a dish of boiled or reconstituted noodles will wonderfully enhance the flavour without seriously raising the fat content.

To prepare deep-fried rice noodles, place the noodles in a large mixing bowl and soak in cold water for 15 minutes. Drain them and lay them on kitchen paper to dry.

Then heat about 1.2 litres/2 pints/5 cups vegetable oil in a large, high-sided frying pan or wok to 180°C/350°F. To test if the oil is ready, carefully drop in a couple of noodle strands. If they puff and curl up immediately, the oil is hot enough. Very carefully, add a handful of dry noodles to the hot oil. As soon as they puff up, after about 2 seconds, flip

Below: Egg noodles are available, dried and fresh, in a wide variety of widths.

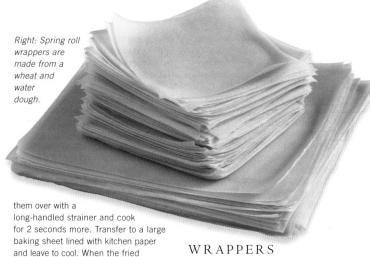

Right: Spring roll wrappers are made from a wheat and water dough.

them over with a long-handled strainer and cook for 2 seconds more. Transfer to a large baking sheet lined with kitchen paper and leave to cool. When the fried noodles are cold they can be transferred to a sealed plastic bag and will stay crisp for about 2 days.

EGG NOODLES

These noodles owe their yellow colour to the egg used in their manufacture. Sold fresh in nests, they must be shaken loose before being cooked. They come in both flat and round shapes. Very thin noodles are known as egg thread noodles. The flat type of noodles are generally used for soups and the rounded type are preferred for stir-frying. Egg noodles freeze well, provided that they are correctly wrapped. Thaw them thoroughly before using them in soup or noodles dishes.

Egg noodles should be cooked in boiling water for 4–5 minutes, or according to the packet instructions. Drain and serve.

CELLOPHANE NOODLES

These thin, wiry noodles, also called glass, jelly or bean thread noodles, are made from mung beans. They are the same size as ordinary egg noodles but they are transparent, resembling strips of cellophane or glass. They are only available dried.

Cellophane noodles are never served on their own, but always as an ingredient in a dish. Soak them in hot water for 10–15 minutes to soften them, then drain and cut into shorter strands.

WRAPPERS

These are made from wheat or rice flour and are used throughout Thailand and South-east Asia to wrap around a filling. Some may be eaten fresh while others are deep-fried.

WONTON WRAPPERS

Originally Chinese, these thin yellow pastry squares are made from egg and wheat flour and can be bought fresh or frozen. Fresh wrappers will last for about five days, double-wrapped and stored in the refrigerator. Simply peel off the number you require. Frozen wrappers should be thawed before use.

RICE PAPER

These brittle, semi-transparent, paper-thin sheets are made from a mixture of rice flour, water and salt, rolled out by a machine until very thin and then dried in the sun. Packets of 50–100 sheets are available. Store in a cool, dry place. Before use, dip in water until pliable, then wrap around a filling to make fresh spring rolls.

SPRING ROLL WRAPPERS

These wafer-thin wrappers are used to make classic spring rolls. The sizes available range from 8cm/3¼in to 30cm/12in square, and they usually come in packets of 20. Once opened, spring roll wrappers will dry out quickly, so peel off one at a time and keep the rest of the wrappers covered.

FISH AND SHELLFISH

Fish is an extremely important source of protein throughout Thailand and South-east Asia, whose many coastal waters, rivers and lakes provide an abundant harvest. From a healthy eating perspective, bass and sea bass, cod, sea bream, sole and plaice are excellent low-fat protein foods, but the darker-fleshed oily fish like tuna, salmon, carp, trout, mackerel, sardines and herring excite even more interest to those in search of a healthy diet. The Omega-3 fatty acids these fish contain benefit the heart. Scientific research has proved that they can help lower cholesterol and triglyceride levels and reduce the risk of high blood pressure. Scallops and squid are also a good source of Omega-3 fatty acids, and these, along with prawns (shrimp), crab and clams are used to great effect by Thai and South-east Asian cooks, whether steamed, poached, baked or fried.

CARP

This freshwater fish is widely farmed in Asia. It has meaty, moist flesh that can taste a little muddy to those unfamiliar with the distinctive taste. When buying carp, ask the fishmonger to remove the scales and strong dorsal fins. A favourite way of cooking carp is to stuff it with ginger and spring onions (scallions) and serve it with a sweet pickle sauce.

MUSSELS

This shellfish is widely used in Thai and Asian cooking. Farmed mussels are now readily available and they are usually relatively free of barnacles. They are generally sold in quantities of 1kg/2¼lb, sufficient for a main course for two or three people. Look for good-size specimens with glossy shells. Discard any that are not closed, or which fail to shut when tapped. Use the back of a short stout knife to scrape away any barnacles, pull away the hairy "beards", then wash the shellfish thoroughly. The best way to cook mussels is to steam them in a small amount of flavoured liquor in a large lidded pan for 3–4 minutes until the shells open. Use finely chopped fresh root ginger, lemon grass, torn lime leaves and some fish sauce to add flavouring to the mussels.

LOBSTER

This luxury shellfish is usually served as a restaurant dish. To cook a live lobster, put it in a pan of ice cold water, cover the pan tightly and bring the water to the boil. The shell will turn bright red and the flesh will be tender and succulent when the lobster is cooked. If you buy a ready-cooked lobster the tail should spring back into a curl when pulled out straight. Try eating lobster with a dip of soy sauce with grated ginger.

Right from top: Freshwater carp, mackerel and grey mullet.

SALMON

The finest wild salmon has a superb flavour and is an excellent low-fat choice being full of Omega-3 acids. It is a costly fish, however, and so it may not be affordable on a regular basis. Responsibly farmed salmon is more economical to buy, and although the flavour is not quite as good as that of wild salmon, it is still delicious. The rosy flesh is beautifully moist and responds very well to being poached or baked, either on its own or with herbs and spices or aromatics. Salmon can take quite robust flavours. Try it with sweet soy sauce and noodles for a quick supper. When buying fresh salmon, have a good fishmonger cut you a chunk from a large salmon for really excellent results; do not use ready-cut steaks.

CRAB

Several varieties of crab are found in Asian waters. Off the coast of Vietnam and Cambodia, the saltwater variety can grow huge, at least 60cm/2ft in diameter. Crab meat has a distinctive taste that goes well with Thai and South-east Asian flavours. A popular Thai soup combines crab with asparagus, and a Vietnamese dish involves steaming lobster and crabs in beer.

Above: Lobster and scallops are good, low-fat health choices.

Above: Raw, unshelled prawns

SCALLOPS

The tender, sweet flesh of this seafood needs very little cooking. Whenever possible, buy scallops fresh. If they are to be used for sashimi, the coral (roe), black stomach and frill must be removed first. In cooked dishes, the coral can be retained and is regarded as a delicacy.

SEA BASS

Characterized by the delicate flavour of its flesh, sea bass is enjoyed throughout Asia. It holds its shape when cooked, and can be grilled (broiled), steamed, baked or barbecued whole. Sea bass fillets taste delicious when they have been marinated, then cooked on a ridged griddle pan. Chunks or strips make a sensational stir-fry.

SHRIMPS AND PRAWNS

If you ask for shrimp in Britain, then you will be given tiny crustaceans, while in the United States, the term is used to describe the larger shellfish which the British refer to as prawns. However, Asian cooks use both words fairly

Right: Cooked prawns are a way of adding protein to a meal without adding fat.

indiscriminately, so check what a recipe requires. Buy raw shellfish whenever possible, and then cook it yourself. This applies to fresh and frozen mixed seafood. If the shellfish are frozen, thaw them slowly and pat them dry before cooking. Since they are low in fat, they are one of the healthiest forms of protein.

SQUID

The cardinal rule with squid is to either cook it very quickly, or simmer it for a long time. Anything in between will result in seafood that is tough and rubbery. Squid is an ideal candidate for stir-frying with flavours like ginger, garlic, spring onion (scallion) and chilli, and it will also make an interesting salad. For a slow-cooked dish, try squid cooked in a clay pot with chillies and noodles.

TUNA

This very large fish is usually sold as steaks, which can be pink or red, depending on the variety. Avoid steaks with heavy discoloration around the bone, or which are brownish and dull-looking. The flesh should be solid and compact. Tuna loses its colour and can become dry when overcooked, so cook it only briefly over high heat, or stew it gently with moist ingredients like tomatoes and peppers.

Fantail prawns/shrimp

1 Remove the heads from the prawns and peel away most of the body shell. Leave a little of the shell to keep the tail intact.

2 Make a tiny incision in the back of each prawn and remove the black intestinal cord.

3 Hold the prepared prawns by the tails and dip lightly in seasoned cornflour (cornstarch), and then in a frothy batter before cooking them in hot oil until the tails, which are free from batter, turn red.

Butterfly prawns/shrimp

Prawns (shrimp) prepared this way cook quickly and curl attractively.

1 Remove the heads and body shells, but leave the tails. Pull out the intestinal cords using tweezers.

2 Make a cut through the belly of each prawn.

3 Gently open out the two halves of the prawn so that they will look like butterfly wings.

FAT AND CALORIE CONTENTS OF FOOD

The figures show the weight of fat (g) and the energy content per 100g (3½oz) of each of the following typical foods used in Thai and South-east Asian cooking. Use the table to help work out the fat content of favourite dishes.

MEATS	fat (g)	Energy kcals/kJ
Beef minced (ground), raw	16.2	225kcal/934kJ
Beef, rump (round) steak, lean only	4.1	125kcal/526kJ
Beef, fillet (tenderloin) steak	8.5	191kcal/799kJ
Chicken, minced (ground), raw	8.5	106kcal/449kJ
Chicken fillet, raw	1.1	106kcal/449kJ
Chicken thighs, without skin, raw	6.0	126kcal/530kJ
Duck, without skin, cooked	9.5	182kcal/765kJ
Lamb leg, lean, cooked	6.3	198kcal/831kJ
Liver, lamb's, raw	6.2	137kcal/575kJ
Pork, average, lean, raw	4.0	123kcal/519kJ
Pork, lean roast	4.0	163kcal/685kJ
Pork, minced (ground), raw	4.0	123kcal/519kJ
Pork, ribs, raw	10.0	114kcal/480kJ
Turkey, meat only, raw	1.6	105kcal/443kJ
Turkey, minced (ground), raw	6.5	170kcal/715kJ

FISH AND SHELLFISH		
Cod, raw	0.7	80kcal/337kJ
Crab meat, raw	0.5	54kcal/230kJ
Mackerel, raw	16.0	221kcal/930kJ
Monkfish, raw	1.5	76kcal/320kJ
Mussels, raw, weight without shells	1.8	74kcal/312kJ
Mussels, raw, weight with shells	0.6	24kcal/98kJ
Oysters, raw	4.2	120kcal/508kJ
Prawns (shrimp)	1.0	76kcal/320kJ
Salmon, steamed	13.0	200kcal/837kJ
Scallops, raw	1.6	105kcal/440kJ
Sardine fillets, grilled	10.4	195kcal/815kJ
Sardines, grilled, weight with bones	6.3	19kcal/497kJ
Sea bass, raw	2.0	97kcal/406kJ
Squid, boiled	1.0	79kcal/330kJ
Swordfish, grilled	5.1	155kcal/649kJ
Tuna, grilled	6.3	184kcal/770kJ

VEGETABLES	fat (g)	Energy kcals/kJ
Asparagus	0.0	12.5kcal/52.5kJ
Aubergine (eggplant)	0.4	15kcal/63kJ
Bamboo shoots	0.0	29kcal/120kJ
Beansprouts	1.6	10kcal/42kJ
(Bell) peppers	0.4	32kcals/128kJ
Beans, fine green	0.0	7kcal/29kJ
Beetroot (beets)	0.1	36kcal/151kJ
Broccoli	0.9	33kcal/138kJ
Carrot	0.3	35kcal/156kJ
Celery	0.2	7kcal/142kJ
Chilli, fresh	0.0	30kcal/120kJ
Chinese leaves (Chinese cabbage)	0.0	8kcal/35kJ
Courgettes (zucchini)	0.4	18kcal74kJ
Cucumber	0.1	10kcal/40kJ
Leek	0.3	20kcal/87kJ
Lotus root, raw	0.0	74kcal/310kJ
Mangetouts (snow peas)	0.4	81kcal/339kJ
Mung beans, cooked	0.1	70kcal/295kJ
Mushrooms, button (white)	0.5	24kcal/100kJ
Mushrooms, shiitake	0.2	55kcal/230kJ
Mushrooms, dried	0.0	56kcal/240kJ
Onion	0.2	36kcal/151kJ
Pak choi (bok choy)	0.0	13kcal/53kJ
Spinach (fresh, cooked)	0.0	20kcal/87kJ
Spring onion (scallion)	0.0	17kcal/83kJ
Sweet potato (peeled, boiled)	0.0	84kcal/358kJ
Water chestnuts	0.0	98kcal/410kJ

NUTS AND SEEDS		
Cashew nuts	48.0	573kcal/2406kJ
Chestnuts	2.7	169kcal/714kJ
Peanuts	26.9	586kcal/2464kJ
Sesame seeds	47.0	507kcal/2113kJ

Below: Red meat such as beef, lamb and pork have a higher quantity of fat per 100g than white meat.

Below: Seafood is a good source of vitamins, minerals and protein. Oily fish contains high levels of Omega-3 fatty acids.

FRUIT	fat (g)	Energy kcals/kJ
Apples, eating	0.1	47kcal/199kJ
Bananas	0.3	95kcal/403kJ
Grapefruit	0.1	30kcal/126kJ
Grapes (green)	0.0	56kcal/235kJ
Lychees	0.1	58kcal/248kJ
Mangoes	0.0	60Kcal/251kJ
Nectarine	0.0	40kcal/169kJ
Oranges	0.1	37kcal/158kJ
Papayas	0	36kcal/153kJ
Peaches	0.0	31kcal/132kJ
Pineapple, fresh	0.0	50kcal/209kJ
Pineapple, canned chunks	0.2	63Kcal/264kJ
Raspberries	0.0	28kcal/117kJ
Star fruit (carambola)	0.0	25Kcal/105kJ
Strawberries	0.0	27kcal/113kJ
Watermelon	0.0	23kcal/95kJ

BEANS, NOODLES, RICE AND TOFU		
Aduki beans, cooked	0.2	123kcal/525kJ
Noodles, cellophane	trace	351kcal/1468kJ
Noodles, egg	0.5	62kcal/264kJ
Noodles, plain wheat	2.5	354kcal/1190kJ
Noodles, rice	0.1	360kcal/1506kJ
Noodles, soba	0.1	99kcal/414kJ
Rice, brown, uncooked	2.8	357kcal/1518kJ
Rice, white, uncooked	3.6	383kcal/1630kJ
Tofu, firm	4.2	73kcal/304kJ
Tofu, silken	2.5	55kcal/230kJ

BAKING AND PANTRY		
Cornflour (cornstarch)	0.7	354kcal/1508kJ
Flour, plain (all-purpose) white	1.3	341kcal/1450kJ
Flour, self-raising (self-rising)	1.2	330kcal/1407kJ
Flour, wholemeal (whole-wheat)	2.2	310kcal/1318kJ
Tapioca	0.0	28kcal/119kJ
Honey	0.0	288kcal/1229kJ
Soy sauce, per 5ml/1 tsp	0.0	9kcal/40kJ
Sugar, white	0.3	94kcal/1680kJ

FATS, OILS AND EGGS	fat (g)	Energy kcals/kJ
Butter	81.7	737kcal/3031kJ
Low-fat spread	40.5	390kcal/1605kJ
Very low-fat spread	25.0	273kcal/1128kJ
Oil, corn, per 1 tbsp/15ml	13.8	124kcal/511kJ
Oil, groundnut (peanut), per 1 tbsp/15ml	14.9	134kcal/552kJ
Oil, sesame seed, per 1 tbsp/15ml	14.9	134kcal/552kJ
Oil, sunflower, per 1 tbsp/15ml	13.8	124kcal/511kJ
Eggs	10.8	147kcal/612kJ
Coconut milk	17.0	225kcal/944kJ
Coconut milk, reduced-fat	8.6	137kcal/575kJ
Coconut cream	68.8	669kcal/2760kJ

DAIRY PRODUCTS		
Cheese, hard	34.4	412kcal/1708kJ
Cheese, hard, reduced fat	15.0	261kcal/1091kJ
Cheese, cottage	3.9	98kcal/413kJ
Cheese, cream	47.4	439kcal/1807kJ
Cream, double (heavy)	48.0	449kcal/1849kJ
Cream, reduced-fat double (heavy)	24.0	243kcal/1002kJ
Cream, single (light)	19.1	198kcal/817kJ
Cream, whipping	39.3	373kcal/1539kJ
Crème fraîche	40.0	379kcal/156kJ
Crème fraîche, reduced fat	15.0	165kcal/683kJ
Fromage frais, plain	7.1	113kcal/469kJ
Fromage frais, very low-fat	0.2	58kcal/247kJ
Milk, full cream (whole)	3.9	66kcal/275kJ
Milk, semi-skimmed (low-fat)	1.5	35kcal/146kJ
Milk, skimmed	0.1	33kcal/130kJ
Yogurt, low-fat natural (plain)	0.8	56kcal/236kJ
Yogurt, Greek (US strained plain)	9.1	115kcal/477kJ

Below: Vegetables are very low in fat. Eat them raw for a filling snack, or steam them to retain maximum nutritional value.

Below: Soya products, such as tofu, soya milk and soya beans, contain isoflavones that are thought to lower cholesterol levels.

SOUPS

In Thailand and South-east Asian countries such as Indonesia and Malaysia soups are more often than not served throughout the meal. They offer a healthy, low-fat flavoursome choice that provides the palate with tastes and textures that complement or contrast with main dishes. Any of these soups are also ideal served for a light lunch or supper — from Hot and Sweet Vegetable and Tofu Soup and Thai Fish Broth to Piquant Prawn Laksa and Beef Noodle Soup there's something for everyone.

SPICY GREEN BEAN SOUP ★

THE BALINESE BASE THIS POPULAR SOUP ON BEANS, BUT ANY SEASONAL VEGETABLES CAN BE ADDED OR SUBSTITUTED. THE RECIPE ALSO INCLUDES SHRIMP PASTE, WHICH IS KNOWN LOCALLY AS TERASI.

2 Finely grind the chopped garlic, macadamia nuts or almonds, shrimp paste and the coriander seeds to a paste using a pestle and mortar or in a food processor.

3 Heat the oil in a wok, and fry the onion until transparent. Remove with a slotted spoon. Add the nut paste to the wok and fry it for 2 minutes without allowing it to brown.

4 Add the reserved vegetable water to the wok and stir well. Add the reduced-fat coconut milk to the wok, bring to the boil and add the bay leaves. Cook the soup, uncovered, for 15–20 minutes.

5 Just before serving, reserve a few green beans, fried onions and beansprouts for garnish and stir the rest into the soup and heat through. Add the lemon wedges, lemon juice and seasoning; stir well. Pour into individual soup bowls and serve, garnished with reserved green beans, onion and beansprouts.

SERVES EIGHT

INGREDIENTS

225g/8oz green beans
1.2 litres/2 pints/5 cups lightly salted water
1 garlic clove, roughly chopped
2 macadamia nuts or 4 almonds, finely chopped
1cm/½ in cube shrimp paste
10–15ml/2–3 tsp coriander seeds, dry fried
15ml/1 tbsp sunflower oil
1 onion, finely sliced
400ml/14fl oz can reduced-fat coconut milk
2 bay leaves
225g/8oz/4 cups beansprouts
8 thin lemon wedges
30ml/2 tbsp lemon juice
salt and ground black pepper

1 Trim the beans, then cut them into small pieces. Bring the lightly salted water to the boil, add the beans to the pan and cook for 3–4 minutes. Drain, reserving the cooking water. Set the beans aside.

COOK'S TIP
Dry fry the coriander seeds for about 2 minutes until the aroma is released.

Energy 51kcal/212kJ; Protein 2.2g; Carbohydrate 5.2g, of which sugars 4.2g; Fat 2.5g, of which saturates 0.4g, of which polyunsaturates 1.2g; Cholesterol 3mg; Calcium 43mg; Fibre 1.2g; Sodium 84mg.

CELLOPHANE NOODLE SOUP ★

THE NOODLES USED IN THIS SOUP GO BY VARIOUS NAMES: GLASS NOODLES, CELLOPHANE NOODLES, BEAN THREAD OR TRANSPARENT NOODLES. THEY ARE ESPECIALLY VALUED FOR THEIR BRITTLE TEXTURE.

SERVES FOUR

INGREDIENTS

4 large dried shiitake mushrooms
15g/½oz dried golden needles
  (lily buds)
½ cucumber, coarsely chopped
2 garlic cloves, halved
90g/3½oz white cabbage, chopped
1.2 litres/2 pints/5 cups boiling water
115g/4oz cellophane noodles
30ml/2 tbsp soy sauce
15ml/1 tbsp palm sugar or light
  muscovado (brown) sugar
90g/3½oz block silken tofu, diced
fresh coriander (cilantro) leaves,
  to garnish

1 Soak the shiitake mushrooms in warm water for 30 minutes. In a separate bowl, soak the dried golden needles in warm water, also for 30 minutes.

2 Meanwhile, put the cucumber, garlic and cabbage in a food processor and process to a smooth paste. Scrape the mixture into a large pan and add the measured boiling water.

3 Bring to the boil, then reduce the heat and cook for 2 minutes, stirring occasionally. Strain this stock into another pan, return to a low heat and bring to simmering point.

4 Drain the golden needles, rinse under cold running water, then drain again. Cut off any hard ends. Add to the stock with the noodles, soy sauce and sugar and cook for 5 minutes more.

5 Strain the mushroom soaking liquid into the soup. Discard the mushroom stems, then slice the caps. Divide them and the tofu among four bowls. Pour the soup over, garnish and serve.

Energy 148kcal/618kJ; Protein 4.1g; Carbohydrate 29.7g, of which sugars 5.7g; Fat 1.1g, of which saturates 0.1g, of which polyunsaturates 0.5g; Cholesterol 0mg; Calcium 139mg; Fibre 0.7g; Sodium 546mg.

OMELETTE SOUP ★

A VERY SATISFYING BUT HEALTHY SOUP THAT IS QUICK AND EASY TO PREPARE. IT IS VERSATILE, TOO, IN THAT YOU CAN VARY THE VEGETABLES ACCORDING TO WHAT IS AVAILABLE.

SERVES FOUR

INGREDIENTS
1 egg
5ml/1 tsp sunflower oil
900ml/1½ pints/3¾ cups
  vegetable stock
2 large carrots, finely diced
4 leaves pak choi (bok choy),
  shredded
30ml/2 tbsp soy sauce
2.5ml/½ tsp granulated sugar
2.5ml/½ tsp ground black pepper
fresh coriander (cilantro) leaves,
  to garnish

VARIATION
Use Savoy cabbage instead of pak choi.
In Thailand there are about forty
different types of pak choi, including
miniature versions.

1 Put the egg in a bowl and beat lightly
with a fork. Heat the oil in a small frying
pan until it is hot, but not smoking.
Pour in the egg and swirl the pan so
that it coats the base evenly. Cook over
a medium heat until the omelette has
set and the underside is golden. Slide
it out of the pan and roll it up like a
pancake. Slice into 5mm/¼in rounds
and set aside for the garnish.

2 Put the stock into a large pan. Add
the carrots and pak choi and bring
to the boil. Reduce the heat and simmer
for 5 minutes, then add the soy sauce,
granulated sugar and pepper.

3 Stir well, then pour into warmed
bowls. Lay a few omelette rounds on the
surface of each portion and complete
the garnish with the coriander leaves.

Energy 52kcal/217kJ; Protein 3.4g; Carbohydrate 4.1g, of which sugars 3.8g; Fat 2.6g, of which saturates 0.6g, of which polyunsaturates 0.9g; Cholesterol 48mg; Calcium 100mg; Fibre 1.7g; Sodium 628mg.

CRAB AND ASPARAGUS SOUP ★

THE VIETNAMESE OFTEN COMBINE ASPARAGUS WITH CRAB AND MAKE A DELICIOUS LOW-FAT SOUP. SERVE THIS SOUP AS A LIGHT LUNCH OR SUPPER WITH PLAIN NOODLES.

SERVES SIX

INGREDIENTS

350g/12oz asparagus spears, trimmed and halved
900ml/1½ pints/3¾ cups chicken stock, preferably home-made
15ml/1 tbsp sunflower oil
6 shallots, chopped
115g/4oz crab meat, fresh or canned, chopped
15ml/1 tbsp cornflour (cornstarch), mixed to a paste with water
30ml/2 tbsp Thai fish sauce
1 egg, lightly beaten
chopped chives, plus extra chives to garnish
salt and ground black pepper to taste

1 Cook the asparagus spears in the chicken stock for 5–6 minutes until tender. Drain, reserving the stock.

2 Heat the oil and stir-fry the shallots for 2 minutes. Add the asparagus spears, crab meat and chicken stock.

3 Bring the mixture to the boil and cook for 3 minutes, then remove the wok or pan from the heat and spoon some of the liquid into the cornflour mixture. Return this to the wok or pan and stir until the soup begins to thicken slightly.

4 Stir in the fish sauce, with salt and pepper to taste, then pour the beaten egg into the soup, stirring briskly so that the egg forms threads. Finally, stir the chopped chives into the soup and serve immediately, garnished with chives.

COOK'S TIP
If fresh asparagus isn't available, use 350g/12oz can asparagus. Drain and halve the spears.

Energy 75kcal/313kJ; Protein 6.6g; Carbohydrate 5.2g, of which sugars 2.4g; Fat 3.3g, of which saturates 0.6g, of which polyunsaturates 1.4g; Cholesterol 46mg; Calcium 49mg; Fibre 1.2g; Sodium 476mg.

PUMPKIN AND COCONUT SOUP ★

IN THIS LOVELY LOOKING SOUP, THE NATURAL SWEETNESS OF THE PUMPKIN IS HEIGHTENED BY THE ADDITION OF A LITTLE SUGAR, BUT THIS IS BALANCED BY THE CHILLIES, SHRIMP PASTE AND DRIED SHRIMP. REDUCED-FAT COCONUT MILK BLURS THE BOUNDARIES BEAUTIFULLY.

SERVES SIX

INGREDIENTS

450g/1lb pumpkin
2 garlic cloves, crushed
4 shallots, finely chopped
2.5ml/½ tsp shrimp paste
1 lemon grass stalk, chopped
2 fresh green chillies, seeded
15ml/1 tbsp dried shrimp soaked
   for 10 minutes in warm water
   to cover
600ml/1 pint/2½ cups
   chicken stock
600ml/1 pint/2½ cups reduced-fat
   coconut milk
30ml/2 tbsp Thai fish sauce
5ml/1 tsp granulated sugar
115g/4oz small cooked shelled
   prawns (shrimp)
salt and ground black pepper
To garnish
2 fresh red chillies, seeded and
   thinly sliced
10–12 fresh basil leaves

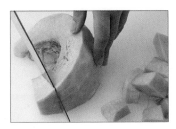

1 Peel the pumpkin and cut it into quarters with a sharp knife. Scoop out the seeds with a teaspoon and discard. Cut the flesh into chunks about 2cm/ ¾in thick and set aside.

2 Put the garlic, shallots, shrimp paste, lemon grass, green chillies and salt to taste in a mortar. Drain the dried shrimp, discarding the soaking liquid, and add them, then use a pestle to grind the mixture into a paste. Alternatively, place all the ingredients in a food processor and process to a paste.

3 Bring the chicken stock to the boil in a large pan. Add the ground paste and stir well to dissolve.

4 Add the pumpkin chunks and bring to a simmer. Simmer for 10–15 minutes, or until the pumpkin is tender.

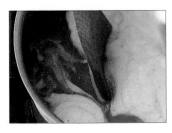

5 Stir in the coconut milk, then bring the soup back to simmering point. Do not let it boil. Add the fish sauce, sugar and ground black pepper to taste.

6 Add the prawns and cook for a further 2–3 minutes, until they are heated through. Serve in warm soup bowls, garnished with chillies and basil leaves.

COOK'S TIP
Shrimp paste is made from ground shrimp fermented in brine.

PRAWN AND PORK SOUP WITH RICE STICKS ★

THIS LOW-FAT AND HEALTHY SOUP IS A SPECIALITY OF HO CHI MINH CITY (FORMERLY SAIGON), WHERE THE PORK STOCK IS ENHANCED WITH THE INTENSE SWEET AND SMOKY FLAVOUR OF DRIED SQUID. IT IS ALSO A POPULAR EVERYDAY SOUP IN CAMBODIA.

SERVES FOUR

INGREDIENTS
225g/8oz lean pork tenderloin
225g/8oz dried rice sticks
  (vermicelli), soaked in lukewarm
  water for 20 minutes
20 prawns (shrimp), shelled
  and deveined
115g/4oz/½ cup beansprouts
2 spring onions (scallions),
  finely sliced
2 green or red Thai chillies, seeded
  and finely sliced
1 garlic clove, finely sliced
1 bunch each coriander (cilantro)
  and basil, stalks removed, leaves
  roughly chopped
1 lime, cut into quarters, and
  nuoc cham, to serve
For the stock
  25g/1oz dried squid
  450g/1lb pork ribs
  1 onion, peeled and quartered
  225g/8oz carrots, peeled and cut
    into chunks
  15ml/1 tbsp *nuoc mam*
  15ml/1 tbsp soy sauce
  6 black peppercorns
  salt

1 To make the stock, soak the dried squid in water for 30 minutes, rinse and drain. Put the ribs in a large pan and cover with approximately 2.5 litres/4½ pints/10 cups water. Bring to the boil, skim off any fat, and add the dried squid with the remaining stock ingredients. Cover the pan and simmer for 1 hour, then skim off any foam or fat and continue to simmer, uncovered, for a further 1½ hours.

2 Strain the stock and check the seasoning. You should have roughly 2 litres/3½ pints/8 cups.

COOK'S TIP
To serve the soup on its own, add bitesize pieces of soaked dried shiitake mushrooms or cubes of firm tofu.

3 Pour the stock into a wok or deep pan and bring to the boil. Reduce the heat, add the pork tenderloin and simmer for 25 minutes. Lift the tenderloin out of the stock, place it on a board and cut it into thin slices. Meanwhile, keep the stock simmering gently over a low heat.

4 Bring a pan of water to the boil. Drain the rice sticks and add to the water. Cook for about 5 minutes, or until tender, separating them with chopsticks if they stick together. Drain the rice sticks and divide them among four warm bowls.

5 Drop the prawns into the simmering stock for 1 minute. Lift them out with a slotted spoon and layer them with the slices of pork on top of the rice sticks. Ladle the hot stock over them and sprinkle with beansprouts, spring onions, chillies, garlic and herbs. Serve each bowl of soup with a wedge of lime to squeeze over it and *nuoc cham* to splash on top.

Energy 234kcal/981kJ; Protein 26.2g; Carbohydrate 24.8g, of which sugars 1.6g; Fat 3.3g, of which saturates 1g, of which polyunsaturates 0.6g; Cholesterol 137mg; Calcium 84mg; Fibre 1.1g; Sodium 681mg.

NORTHERN PRAWN AND SQUASH SOUP ★

AS THE TITLE OF THE RECIPE SUGGESTS, THIS COMES FROM NORTHERN THAILAND. IT IS QUITE HEARTY, SOMETHING OF A CROSS BETWEEN A SOUP AND A STEW. THE BANANA FLOWER ISN'T ESSENTIAL, BUT IT DOES ADD A UNIQUE AND AUTHENTIC FLAVOUR.

SERVES FOUR

INGREDIENTS

1 butternut squash, about 300g/11oz
1 litre/1¾ pints/4 cups
   vegetable stock
90g/3½oz/scant 1 cup green beans,
   cut into 2.5cm/1in pieces
45g/1¾oz dried banana
   flower (optional)
15ml/1 tbsp Thai fish sauce
225g/8oz raw prawns (shrimp)
small bunch fresh basil
cooked rice, to serve
For the chilli paste
115g/4oz shallots, sliced
10 drained bottled green peppercorns
1 small fresh green chilli, seeded and
   finely chopped
2.5ml/½ tsp shrimp paste

1 Peel the squash and cut it in half. Scoop out the seeds and discard, then cut the flesh into neat cubes. Set aside.

2 Make the chilli paste by pounding the sliced shallots, peppercorns, chilli and shrimp paste together using a mortar and pestle or puréeing them in a spice blender.

3 Heat the vegetable stock gently in a large pan, then stir in the chilli paste. Add the squash, beans and banana flower, if using. Bring to the boil and cook for 15 minutes.

4 Add the fish sauce, prawns and basil. Simmer for 3 minutes. Serve in warmed bowls, accompanied by rice.

Energy 73kcal/307kJ; Protein 11.8g; Carbohydrate 5.2g, of which sugars 3.9g; Fat 0.7g, of which saturates 0.2g, of which polyunsaturates 0.2g; Cholesterol 113mg; Calcium 90mg; Fibre 1.7g; Sodium 669mg.

HOT-AND-SOUR FISH SOUP ⋆

This tangy soup is found throughout Asia — with the balance of hot, sweet and sour flavours varying from Cambodia to Vietnam. Chillies provide the heat, tamarind produces the tartness and the delicious sweetness comes from pineapple.

SERVES FOUR

INGREDIENTS
1 catfish, sea bass or red snapper,
  about 1kg/2¼lb, filleted
30ml/2 tbsp *nuoc mam*
2 garlic cloves, finely chopped
25g/1oz dried squid, soaked in water
  for 30 minutes
10ml/2 tsp vegetable oil
2 spring onions (scallions), sliced
2 shallots, sliced
4cm/1½in fresh root ginger, peeled
  and chopped
2–3 lemon grass stalks, cut into
  strips and crushed
30ml/2 tbsp tamarind paste
2–3 Thai chillies, seeded and sliced
15ml/1 tbsp sugar
30–45ml/2–3 tbsp *nuoc mam*
225g/8oz fresh pineapple, peeled
  and diced
3 tomatoes, skinned, seeded and
  roughly chopped
50g/2oz canned sliced bamboo
  shoots, drained
1 small bunch fresh coriander
  (cilantro), stalks removed, leaves
  finely chopped
salt and ground black pepper
115g/4oz/½cup beansprouts and
  1 bunch dill, fronds roughly
  chopped, to garnish
1 lime, cut into quarters, to serve

1 Cut the fish into bitesize pieces, mix with the *nuoc mam* and garlic and leave to marinate. Save the head, tail and bones for the stock. Drain and rinse the soaked dried squid.

2 Heat the oil in a deep pan and stir in the spring onions, shallots, ginger, lemon grass and dried squid. Add the reserved fish head, tail and bones, and sauté them gently for a minute or two. Pour in 1.2 litres/2 pints/5 cups water and bring to the boil. Reduce the heat and simmer for 30 minutes.

3 Strain the stock into another deep pan and bring to the boil. Stir in the tamarind paste, chillies, sugar and *nuoc mam* and simmer for 2–3 minutes. Add the pineapple, tomatoes and bamboo shoots and simmer for a further 2–3 minutes. Stir in the fish pieces and the chopped fresh coriander, and cook until the fish turns opaque.

4 Season to taste and ladle the soup into hot bowls. Garnish with beansprouts and dill, and serve with the lime quarters to squeeze over.

VARIATIONS
• Depending on your mood, or your palate, you can adjust the balance of hot and sour by adding more chilli or tamarind to taste. Enjoyed as a meal in itself, the soup is usually served with plain steamed rice but in Ho Chi Minh City in Vietnam it is served with chunks of fresh baguette, which are perfect for soaking up the spicy, fruity, tangy broth.
• Other fresh herbs, such as chopped mint and basil leaves, also complement this soup.

Energy 166kcal/704kJ; Protein 23.1g; Carbohydrate 10.9g, of which sugars 10g; Fat 3.7g, of which saturates 0.6g, of which polyunsaturates 1.7g; Cholesterol 51mg; Calcium 113mg; Fibre 3g; Sodium 116mg.

THAI FISH BROTH ★

LEMON GRASS, CHILLIES AND GALANGAL ARE AMONG THE FLAVOURINGS USED IN THIS FRAGRANT SOUP.

SERVES THREE

INGREDIENTS

1 litre/1¾ pints/4 cups fish or
  light chicken stock
4 lemon grass stalks
3 limes
2 small fresh hot red chillies,
  seeded and thinly sliced
2cm/¾in piece fresh galangal,
  peeled and thinly sliced
6 fresh coriander (cilantro) stalks
2 kaffir lime leaves,
  finely chopped
350g/12oz monkfish fillet, skinned
  and cut into 2.5cm/1in pieces
15ml/1 tbsp rice vinegar
45ml/3 tbsp Thai fish sauce
30ml/2 tbsp chopped coriander
  (cilantro) leaves, to garnish

1 Pour the stock into a pan and bring it to the boil. Meanwhile, slice the bulb end of each lemon grass stalk diagonally into pieces about 3mm/⅛in thick. Peel off four wide strips of lime rind with a potato peeler, taking care to avoid the white pith underneath which would make the soup bitter. Squeeze the limes and reserve the juice.

2 Add the sliced lemon grass, lime rind, chillies, galangal and coriander stalks to the stock, with the kaffir lime leaves. Simmer for 1–2 minutes.

VARIATIONS

Prawns (shrimp), scallops, squid or sole can be substituted for the monkfish. If you use kaffir lime leaves, you will need the juice of only 2 limes.

3 Add the monkfish, rice vinegar and Thai fish sauce, with half the reserved lime juice. Simmer for about 3 minutes, until the fish is just cooked. Lift out and discard the coriander stalks, taste the broth and add more lime juice if necessary; the soup should taste quite sour. Sprinkle with the coriander leaves and serve very hot.

Energy 88kcal/373kJ; Protein 19.2g; Carbohydrate 1.5g, of which sugars 1.3g; Fat 0.6g, of which saturates 0.1g, of which polyunsaturates 0.2g; Cholesterol 16mg; Calcium 40mg; Fibre 0.4g; Sodium 1112mg

BAMBOO SHOOT, FISH AND RICE SOUP ★

THIS IS A REFRESHING SOUP MADE WITH FRESHWATER FISH SUCH AS CARP OR CATFISH.

SERVES FOUR

INGREDIENTS

- 75g/3oz/scant ½ cup long grain rice, well rinsed
- 250ml/8fl oz/1 cup reduced-fat coconut milk
- 30ml/2 tbsp *tuk prahoc*
- 2 lemon grass stalks, trimmed and crushed
- 25g/1oz galangal, thinly sliced
- 2–3 Thai chillies
- 4 garlic cloves, crushed
- 15ml/1 tbsp palm sugar
- 1 fresh bamboo shoot, peeled, boiled in water for 10 minutes, and sliced
- 450g/1lb freshwater fish fillets, such as carp or catfish, skinned and cut into bitesize pieces
- 1 small bunch fresh basil leaves
- 1 small bunch fresh coriander (cilantro), chopped, and 1 chilli, finely sliced, to garnish
- rice or noodles, to serve

For the stock

- 450g/1lb pork ribs
- 1 onion, quartered
- 225g/8oz carrots, cut into chunks
- 25g/1oz dried squid or dried shrimp, soaked in water for 30 minutes, rinsed and drained
- 15ml/1 tbsp *nuoc mam*
- 15ml/1 tbsp soy sauce
- 6 black peppercorns
- salt

1 To prepare the stock, put the ribs in a large pan and cover with 2.5 litres/ 4¼ pints/10 cups water. Bring to the boil, skim off any fat, and add the remaining stock ingredients. Cover the pan and simmer for 1 hour, then skim off any foam or fat.

2 Simmer the stock, uncovered, for a further 1–1½ hours, until it has reduced. Check the seasoning and strain the stock into another pan. There should be approximately 2 litres/3½ pints/7¾ cups of stock.

3 Bring the pan of stock to the boil. Stir in the rice and reduce the heat. Add the coconut milk, *tuk prahoc*, lemon grass, galangal, chillies, garlic and sugar. Simmer for about 10 minutes to let the flavours mingle. The rice should be just cooked, with bite to it.

4 Add the sliced bamboo shoot and the pieces of fish. Simmer for 5 minutes, until the fish is cooked. Check the seasoning and stir in the basil leaves. Ladle the soup into bowls, garnish with the chopped coriander and chilli, and serve with the rice or noodles.

Energy 269kcal/1130kJ; Protein 35.5g; Carbohydrate 23.2g, of which sugars 7.9g; Fat 3.8g, of which saturates 1.1g, of which polyunsaturates 0.9g; Cholesterol 87mg; Calcium 109mg; Fibre 2.6g; Sodium 214mg

GINGER, CHICKEN <u>AND</u> COCONUT SOUP ★

THIS AROMATIC SOUP IS RICH WITH COCONUT MILK AND INTENSELY FLAVOURED WITH GALANGAL, LEMON GRASS AND KAFFIR LIME LEAVES.

SERVES SIX

INGREDIENTS
4 lemon grass stalks, roots trimmed
2 × 400ml/14fl oz cans reduced-fat
  coconut milk
475ml/16fl oz/2 cups chicken stock
2.5cm/1in piece galangal, peeled and
  thinly sliced
10 black peppercorns, crushed
10 kaffir lime leaves, torn
300g/11oz chicken breast fillets,
  cut into thin strips
115g/4oz/1 cup button (white)
  mushrooms
50g/2oz/½ cup baby corn cobs,
  quartered lengthways
60ml/4 tbsp lime juice
45ml/3 tbsp Thai fish sauce
fresh red chillies, spring onions and
  fresh coriander (cilantro), to garnish

1 Cut off the lower 5cm/2in from each lemon grass stalk and chop it finely. Bruise the remaining pieces of stalk. Bring the coconut milk and chicken stock to the boil in a large pan. Add all the lemon grass, the galangal, peppercorns and half the lime leaves, lower the heat and simmer gently for 10 minutes. Strain into a clean pan.

2 Return the soup to the heat, then add the chicken, mushrooms and corn. Simmer for 5–7 minutes or until the chicken is cooked.

3 Stir in the lime juice and Thai fish sauce, then add the remaining lime leaves. Serve hot, garnished with chopped chillies, spring onions and coriander.

HOT-AND-SOUR PRAWN SOUP ★

THIS IS A CLASSIC THAI SEAFOOD SOUP – TOM YAM KUNG – AND IT IS PROBABLY THE MOST POPULAR AND WELL-KNOWN SOUP FROM THAT COUNTRY.

SERVES SIX

INGREDIENTS
450g/1lb raw king prawns (jumbo
  shrimp), thawed if frozen
1 litre/1¾ pints/4 cups chicken
  stock or water
3 lemon grass stalks, root trimmed
10 kaffir lime leaves, torn in half
225g/8oz can straw mushrooms
45ml/3 tbsp Thai fish sauce
60ml/4 tbsp lime juice
30ml/2 tbsp chopped spring onion
  (scallion)
15ml/1 tbsp fresh coriander
  (cilantro) leaves
4 fresh red chillies, seeded
  and thinly sliced
salt and ground black pepper

1 Shell the prawns, putting the shells in a colander. Devein and set aside.

2 Rinse the shells under cold water to remove all grit and sand, then put in a large pan with the chicken stock or water. Bring to the boil.

3 Bruise the lemon grass stalks with a pestle or mallet and add them to the stock with half the lime leaves. Simmer gently for 5–6 minutes, until the stock is fragrant.

4 Strain the stock, return it to the clean pan and reheat. Add the drained mushrooms and the prawns, then cook until the prawns turn pink.

5 Stir in the Thai fish sauce, lime juice, spring onion, coriander, chillies and the remaining lime leaves. Taste and adjust the seasoning. The soup should be sour, salty, spicy and hot.

Top: Energy 90kcal/383kJ; Protein 13.2g; Carbohydrate 7.4g, of which sugars 7.2g; Fat 1.1g, of which saturates 0.4g, of which polyunsaturates 0.2g; Cholesterol 35mg; Calcium 44mg; Fibre 0.3g; Sodium 807mg.
Bottom: Energy 69kcal/292kJ; Protein 14.5g; Carbohydrate 1.1g, of which sugars 1g; Fat 0.8g, of which saturates 0.1g, of which polyunsaturates 0.2g; Cholesterol 146mg; Calcium 81mg; Fibre 0.9g; Sodium 682mg.

CHICKEN RICE SOUP WITH LEMON GRASS ★

THIS IS CAMBODIA'S ANSWER TO THE CHICKEN NOODLE SOUP THAT IS POPULAR IN THE WEST. LIGHT AND FAT-FREE, THIS TANGY AND DELICIOUS SOUP IS THE PERFECT CHOICE FOR A HOT DAY, AS WELL AS A GREAT PICK-ME-UP WHEN YOU ARE FEELING LOW OR TIRED.

SERVES FOUR

INGREDIENTS

2 lemon grass stalks, trimmed, cut into 3 pieces, and lightly bruised
15ml/1 tbsp Thai fish sauce
90g/3½oz/½ cup short grain rice, rinsed
1 small bunch coriander (cilantro) leaves, finely chopped, and 1 green or red chilli, seeded and cut into thin strips, to garnish
1 lime, cut in wedges, to serve
sea salt
ground black pepper

For the stock

1 small chicken or 2 meaty chicken legs
1 onion, quartered
2 cloves garlic, crushed
25g/1oz fresh root ginger, sliced
2 lemon grass stalks, cut in half lengthways and bruised
2 dried red chillies
30ml/2 tbsp *nuoc mam*

1 Put the chicken into a deep pan. Add all the other stock ingredients and pour in 2 litres/3½ pints/7¾ cups water. Bring to the boil for a few minutes, then reduce the heat and simmer gently with the lid on for 2 hours.

2 Skim off any fat from the stock, strain and reserve. Remove the skin from the chicken and shred the meat. Set aside.

3 Pour the stock back into the deep pan and bring to the boil. Reduce the heat and stir in the lemon grass stalks and fish sauce. Stir in the rice and simmer, uncovered, for about 40 minutes. Add the shredded chicken and season to taste.

4 Ladle the piping hot soup into warmed individual bowls, garnish with chopped coriander and the thin strips of chilli and serve with lime wedges to squeeze over.

COOK'S TIPS

• The fresh, citrus aroma of lemon grass and lime, combined with the warmth of the chillies, is invigorating and awakens the senses. However, many Vietnamese and Cambodians often spike the soup with additional chillies as a garnish, or served on the side.
• Variations of this soup crop up all over Cambodia and Vietnam, where it is often served as a meal in itself.

Energy 194kcal/817kJ; Protein 26.2g; Carbohydrate 18.4g, of which sugars 0.3g; Fat 1.6g, of which saturates 0.3g, of which polyunsaturates 0.2g; Cholesterol 70mg; Calcium 36mg; Fibre 0.6g; Sodium 268mg.

AROMATIC BROTH WITH ROAST DUCK, PAK CHOI AND EGG NOODLES ★

SERVED ON ITS OWN, THIS CHINESE-INSPIRED DUCK AND NOODLE SOUP MAKES A DELICIOUS AUTUMN OR WINTER MEAL. IN A VIETNAMESE HOUSEHOLD, A BOWL OF WHOLE FRESH OR MARINATED CHILLIES MIGHT BE PRESENTED AS A FIERY SIDE DISH TO CHEW ON.

SERVES SIX

INGREDIENTS

5ml/1 tsp sunflower oil
2 shallots, thinly sliced
4cm/1½ in fresh root ginger,
  peeled and sliced
15ml/1 tbsp soy sauce
5ml/1 tsp five-spice powder
10ml/2 tsp sugar
175g/6oz pak choi (bok choy)
450g/1lb fresh egg noodles
225g/8oz roast duck, thinly sliced
sea salt
For the stock
1 chicken carcass
2 carrots, peeled and quartered
2 onions, peeled and quartered
4cm/1½ in fresh root ginger, peeled
  and cut into chunks
2 lemon grass stalks, chopped
30ml/2 tbsp *nuoc mam*
15ml/1 tbsp soy sauce
6 black peppercorns
For the garnish
4 spring onions (scallions), sliced
1–2 red Serrano chillies, seeded and
  finely sliced
1 bunch each coriander (cilantro) and
  basil, stalks removed, leaves
  chopped

1 To make the stock, put the chicken carcass into a deep pan. Add all the other stock ingredients and pour in 2.5 litres/4½ pints/10¼ cups water. Bring to the boil, and boil for a few minutes, skim off any foam, then reduce the heat and simmer gently with the lid on for 2–3 hours. Remove the lid and continue to simmer for a further 30 minutes to reduce the stock. Skim off any fat, season with salt, then strain the stock. Measure out 2 litres/3½ pints/8 cups.

2 Heat the oil in a wok or deep pan and stir in the shallots and ginger. Add the soy sauce, five-spice powder, sugar and stock and bring to the boil. Season with a little salt, reduce the heat and simmer for 10–15 minutes.

3 Meanwhile, cut the pak choi diagonally into wide strips and blanch in boiling water to soften them. Drain and refresh under cold running water to prevent them cooking any further. Bring a large pan of water to the boil, then add the fresh noodles. Cook for 5 minutes, then drain well.

4 Divide the noodles among six soup bowls, lay some of the pak choi and sliced duck over them, and then ladle over generous amounts of the simmering broth. Garnish with the spring onions, chillies and herbs, and serve immediately.

COOK'S TIP
If you can't find fresh egg noodles, substitute dried egg noodles instead. Soak the dried noodles in lukewarm water for 20 minutes, then cook, one portion at a time, in a sieve (strainer) lowered into the boiling water. Use a chopstick to untangle them as they soften. Ready-cooked egg noodles are also available in supermarkets.

Energy 337kcal/1411kJ; Protein 12.1g; Carbohydrate 62.5g, of which sugars 1.1g; Fat 3.3g, of which saturates 0.8g, of which polyunsaturates 0.9g; Cholesterol 41mg; Calcium 66mg; Fibre 0.7g; Sodium 269mg.

C
G

SUR
THE

MAKE

INGR
1 p
ro
30
m
abo
cori
cuc
ma
For the
15m
1 sm
1cm,
pee
1 gar
2.5m
1 larg
cool
fine
50g/2
light
50g/2
5–10n
15ml/
(cilar
squee
salt

1 Heat the
onion, ginge
until the on
chilli powde
stir in the p
Sprinkle with
aside to coo
coriander, le

Energy 44kcal/186

APPETIZERS AND LIGHT BITES

Follow the low-fat recipes in this section and treat your party guests to such delicious healthy snacks as Corn Fritters, Fish Cakes with Cucumber Relish and succulent Salt and Pepper Prawns. Traditional street fare such as spring rolls, fritters and samosas can be amazingly low in cholesterol and prove a healthy-eating choice. Garlic, ginger, coriander, chillies and vegetables combine to make appetizers and light bites that are both irresistible and delicious.

FISH CAKES WITH CUCUMBER RELISH ★

THESE WONDERFUL SMALL FISH CAKES ARE A VERY FAMILIAR AND POPULAR APPETIZER IN THAILAND AND INCREASINGLY THROUGHOUT SOUTH-EAST ASIA. THEY ARE USUALLY SERVED WITH THAI BEER.

MAKES ABOUT TWELVE

INGREDIENTS
5 kaffir lime leaves
300g/11oz cod, cut into chunks
30ml/2 tbsp red curry paste
1 egg
30ml/2 tbsp Thai fish sauce
5ml/1 tsp sugar
30ml/2 tbsp cornflour (cornstarch)
15ml/1 tbsp chopped fresh
  coriander (cilantro)
50g/2oz green beans, finely sliced
spray vegetable oil, for frying
Chinese mustard cress,
  to garnish
For the cucumber relish
60ml/4 tbsp coconut or rice vinegar
50g/2oz/¼ cup sugar
1 head pickled garlic
15ml/1 tbsp fresh root ginger
1 cucumber, cut into matchsticks
4 shallots, finely sliced

1 Make the cucumber relish. Bring the vinegar and sugar to the boil in a small pan with 60ml/4 tbsp water, stirring until the sugar has dissolved. Remove from the heat and cool.

2 Separate the pickled garlic into cloves. Chop these finely along with the ginger and place in a bowl. Add the cucumber and shallots, pour over the vinegar mixture and mix lightly.

3 Reserve two kaffir lime leaves for garnish and thinly slice the remainder. Put the chunks of fish, curry paste and egg in a food processor and process to a smooth paste. Transfer the mixture to a bowl and stir in the fish sauce, sugar, cornflour, sliced kaffir lime leaves, coriander and green beans. Mix well, then shape the mixture into about twelve 5mm/¼in thick cakes, measuring about 5cm/2in in diameter.

4 Spray the oil in a non-stick wok or deep-frying pan. Fry the fish cakes, a few at a time, for about 4–5 minutes until cooked and evenly brown.

5 Lift out the fish cakes and drain them on kitchen paper. Keep each batch hot while frying successive batches. Garnish with the reserved kaffir leaves and Chinese mustard cress. Serve with the cucumber relish.

Energy 54kcal/228kJ; Protein 5.4g; Carbohydrate 6.4g, of which sugars 5g; Fat 0.9g, of which saturates 0.2g, of which polyunsaturates 0.2g; Cholesterol 27mg; Calcium 12mg; Fibre 0.2g; Sodium 22mg.

GREEN CURRY PUFFS ★

SHRIMP PASTE AND GREEN CURRY SAUCE, USED JUDICIOUSLY, GIVE THESE PUFFS THEIR DISTINCTIVE, SPICY, SAVOURY FLAVOUR, AND THE ADDITION OF CHILLI STEPS UP THE HEAT.

MAKES TWENTY-FOUR

INGREDIENTS

24 small wonton wrappers, about
  8cm/3¼in square, thawed if frozen
15ml/1 tbsp cornflour (cornstarch),
  mixed to a paste with 30ml/
  2 tbsp water
5ml/1 tsp sunflower oil
For the filling
1 small potato, about 115g/4oz,
  boiled and mashed
25g/1oz/3 tbsp cooked petits pois
  (baby peas)
25g/1oz/3 tbsp cooked corn
few sprigs fresh coriander
  (cilantro), chopped
1 small fresh red chilli, seeded and
  finely chopped
½ lemon grass stalk, finely chopped
15ml/1 tbsp soy sauce
5ml/1 tsp shrimp paste or fish sauce
5ml/1 tsp Thai green curry paste

1 Combine the filling ingredients. Lay out one wonton wrapper and place a teaspoon of the filling in the centre.

2 Brush a little of the cornflour paste along two sides of the square. Fold the other two sides over to meet them, then press together to make a triangular pastry and seal in the filling. Make more pastries in the same way, thinning the paste with a little water if it becomes too thick.

3 Preheat the oven to 240°C/475°F/ Gas 9 and prepare a non-stick baking tray or line a baking tray with baking parchment. Lightly whisk the egg white with the oil and 5ml/1 tsp water.

4 Brush the pastries generously with the egg white and place on the baking sheet. Bake for about 5–8 minutes, until browned and crisp. If you intend serving the puffs hot, place them in a low oven while cooking successive batches. The puffs also taste good cold.

COOK'S TIP
Wonton wrappers dry out quickly, so keep them covered, using clear film (plastic wrap), until you are ready to use them.

Energy 32kcal/134kJ; Protein 1g; Carbohydrate 6.7g, of which sugars 0.4g; Fat 0.3g, of which saturates 0g, of which polyunsaturates 0.1g; Cholesterol 1mg; Calcium 16mg; Fibre 0.4g; Sodium 58mg.

FIRECRACKERS ★

IT'S EASY TO SEE HOW THESE PASTRY-WRAPPED PRAWN SNACKS GOT THEIR NAME (KRATHAK IN THAI)
SINCE AS WELL AS RESEMBLING FIREWORKS, THEIR CONTENTS EXPLODE WITH FLAVOUR.

2 Mix the curry paste with the fish sauce in a shallow dish. Add the prawns and turn them in the mixture until they are well coated. Cover and leave to marinate for 10 minutes.

3 Place a wonton wrapper on the work surface at an angle so that it forms a diamond shape, then fold the top corner over so that the point is in the centre. Place a prawn, slits down, on the wrapper, with the tail projecting from the folded end, then fold the bottom corner over the other end of the prawn.

4 Fold each side of the wrapper over in turn to make a tightly folded roll. Tie a noodle in a bow around the roll and set it aside. Repeat with the remaining prawns and wrappers.

5 Preheat the oven to 240°C/475°F/ Gas 9. Prepare a non-stick baking sheet or line a baking sheet with baking parchment. Lightly whisk the egg white with the oil and 5ml/1 tsp water. Brush the wrapped prawns generously with egg white, so they are well moistened, and place on the baking sheet. Bake for 5–6 minutes, until crisp and lightly browned.

MAKES SIXTEEN

INGREDIENTS
  16 large, raw king prawns (jumbo
    shrimp), heads and shells removed
    but tails left on
  5ml/1 tsp red curry paste
  15ml/1 tbsp Thai fish sauce
  16 small wonton wrappers, about
    8cm/3¼in square, thawed if frozen
  16 fine egg noodles, soaked
    (see Cook's Tip)
  1 egg white
  5ml/1 tsp sunflower oil

1 Place the prawns on their sides and cut two slits through the underbelly of each, one about 1cm/½in from the head end and the other about 1cm/½in from the first cut, cutting across the prawn. This will prevent the prawns from curling when they are cooked.

COOK'S TIP
Soak the fine egg noodles used as ties for the prawn rolls in a bowl of boiling water for 2–3 minutes, until softened, then drain, refresh under cold running water and drain well again.

Energy 37kcal/155kJ; Protein 2.1g; Carbohydrate 6g, of which sugars 0.2g; Fat 0.6g, of which saturates 0.1g, of which polyunsaturates 0.2g; Cholesterol 13mg; Calcium 13mg; Fibre 0.2g; Sodium 88mg.

CHA GIO AND NUOC CHAM ★★

CHINESE SPRING ROLL WRAPPERS ARE USED HERE INSTEAD OF THE RICE PAPERS TRADITIONALLY USED IN VIETNAM AND THE PHILIPPINES. CHA GIO IS AN IMMENSELY POPULAR SNACK IN VIETNAM.

MAKES FIFTEEN

INGREDIENTS
25g/1oz cellophane noodles soaked
   for 10 minutes in hot water to cover
6–8 dried cloud ear (wood ear),
   mushrooms soaked for 30 minutes
   in warm water to cover
225g/8oz minced (ground) lean pork
225g/8oz fresh or canned crab meat
4 spring onions (scallions), trimmed
   and finely chopped
5ml/1 tsp Thai fish sauce
flour and water paste, to seal
250g/9oz packet spring roll wrappers
1 egg white
5ml/1 tsp sunflower oil
salt and ground black pepper
For the *nuoc cham* sauce
2 fresh red chillies, seeded and
   pounded to a paste
2 garlic cloves, crushed
15ml/1 tbsp sugar
45ml/3 tbsp Thai fish sauce
juice of 1 lime or ½ lemon

2 Mix the noodles and the cloud ears with the pork and set aside. Remove any cartilage from the crab meat and add to the pork mixture with the spring onions and fish sauce. Season to taste, mixing well.

3 Place a spring roll wrapper in front of you, diamond-fashion. Spoon some mixture just below the centre, fold over the nearest point and roll once.

4 Fold in the sides to enclose, brush the edges with flour paste and roll up to seal. Repeat with the remaining wrappers.

5 Preheat the oven to 200°C/400F/Gas 6. Whisk the egg white with the oil and 5ml/ 1 tsp water. Brush the rolls generously with egg white, and place on a non-stick baking sheet. Bake for 25–30 minutes, until crisp and brown. To eat, dip the hot rolls in the *nuoc cham* sauce.

1 Make the *nuoc cham* sauce by mixing the chillies, garlic, sugar and fish sauce in a bowl and stirring in lime or lemon juice to taste. Drain the noodles and snip into 2.5cm/1in lengths. Drain the cloud ears, trim away any rough stems and slice the wood ears finely.

COOK'S TIP
Serve the rolls Vietnamese-style by wrapping each roll in a lettuce leaf with a few sprigs of fresh mint and coriander (cilantro) and a stick of cucumber.

Energy 133kcal/558kJ; Protein 11.1g; Carbohydrate 10g, of which sugars 0.4g; Fat 5.7g, of which saturates 0.7g, of which polyunsaturates 2.6g; Cholesterol 36mg; Calcium 21mg; Fibre 0.5g; Sodium 211mg.

SOFT-SHELL CRABS WITH CHILLI AND SALT ★★

IF FRESH SOFT-SHELL CRABS ARE UNAVAILABLE, YOU CAN BUY FROZEN ONES IN ASIAN SUPERMARKETS.
ALLOW TWO SMALL CRABS PER SERVING, OR ONE IF THEY ARE LARGE.

SERVES FOUR

INGREDIENTS
    8 small soft-shell crabs, thawed
        if frozen
    50g/2oz/½ cup plain
        (all-purpose) flour
    15ml/1 tbsp sunflower oil
    2 large fresh red chillies, or
        1 green and 1 red, seeded and
        thinly sliced
    4 spring onions (scallions) or a
        small bunch of garlic chives,
        chopped
    coarse sea salt and ground
        black pepper
To serve
    shredded lettuce, mooli (daikon)
        and carrot
    light soy sauce

1 Pat the crabs dry with kitchen paper. Season the flour with pepper and coat the crabs lightly with the mixture.

2 Heat the oil in a shallow pan until very hot, then put in the crabs (you may need to do this in two batches). Fry for 2–3 minutes on each side, until the crabs are golden brown but still juicy in the middle. Drain the cooked crabs on kitchen paper and keep hot.

3 Add the sliced chillies and spring onions or garlic chives to the oil remaining in the pan and cook gently for about 2 minutes. Sprinkle over a generous pinch of salt, then spread the mixture on to the crabs.

4 Mix the shredded lettuce, mooli and carrot together. Arrange on plates, top each portion with two crabs and serve, with light soy sauce for dipping.

Energy 133kcal/558kJ; Protein 11.1g; Carbohydrate 10g, of which sugars 0.4g; Fat 5.7g, of which saturates 0.7g, of which polyunsaturates 2.6g; Cholesterol 36mg; Calcium 21mg; Fibre 0.5g; Sodium 211mg.

SALT AND PEPPER PRAWNS ★

THESE SUCCULENT SHELLFISH BEG TO BE EATEN SIZZLINGLY HOT WITH THE FINGERS, SO PROVIDE FINGER BOWLS OR HOT CLOTHS FOR YOUR GUESTS.

SERVES FOUR

INGREDIENTS
15–18 large raw prawns (shrimp),
  in the shell, about 450g/1lb
15ml/1 tbsp sunflower oil
3 shallots or 1 small onion,
  very finely chopped
2 garlic cloves, crushed
1cm/½in piece fresh root
  ginger, peeled and very
  finely grated
1–2 fresh red chillies, seeded and
  finely sliced
2.5ml/½ tsp sugar or
  to taste
3–4 spring onions (scallions),
  shredded, to garnish
For the fried salt
  10ml/2 tsp salt
  5ml/1 tsp Sichuan peppercorns

2 Carefully remove the heads and legs from the raw prawns and discard. Leave the body shells and the tails in place. Pat dry with sheets of kitchen paper.

3 Heat the oil in a shallow pan until very hot. Fry the prawns for 2–3 minutes each side until cooked through, then lift them out and drain thoroughly on kitchen paper.

4 Reheat the oil in the frying pan. Add the fried salt, together with the shallots or onion, garlic, ginger, chillies and sugar. Toss together for 1 minute, then add the prawns and toss them over the heat for 1 minute more until they are coated and the shells are impregnated with the seasonings. Serve immediately, garnished with the spring onions.

1 Make the fried salt by dry frying the salt and peppercorns in a heavy frying pan over medium heat until the peppercorns begin to release their aroma. Leave the mixture until cool, then tip it into a mortar and crush it with a pestle.

COOK'S TIP
"Fried salt" is also known as "Cantonese salt" or simply "salt and pepper mix". It is widely used as a table condiment or as a dip for deep fried or roasted food, but can also be an ingredient in a recipe, as here. Black or white peppercorns can be substituted for the Sichuan peppercorns. For the best flavour it really is best made when required.

Energy 122kcal/514kJ; Protein 20.1g; Carbohydrate 2.7g, of which sugars 2.4g; Fat 3.5g, of which saturates 0.5g, of which polyunsaturates 1.9g; Cholesterol 219mg; Calcium 97mg; Fibre 0.3g; Sodium 1197mg.

PAN-STEAMED MUSSELS <u>WITH</u> LEMON GRASS, CHILLI <u>AND</u> THAI HERBS ★

LIKE SO MANY THAI DISHES, THIS IS VERY EASY TO PREPARE AND VERY LOW IN FAT. THE LEMON GRASS AND KAFFIR LIME LEAVES ADD A REFRESHING TANG TO THE MUSSELS.

SERVES SIX

INGREDIENTS
    500g/1¼lb fresh mussels
    1 lemon grass stalk, finely chopped
    2 shallots, chopped
    2 kaffir lime leaves, coarsely torn
    1 fresh red chilli, sliced
    15ml/1 tbsp Thai fish sauce
    30ml/2 tbsp fresh lime juice
    thinly sliced spring onions (scallions)
        and coriander (cilantro) leaves,
        to garnish

1 Clean the mussels by pulling off the beards, scrubbing the shells well and removing any barnacles. Discard any mussels that are broken or which do not close when tapped sharply.

2 Place the mussels in a large, heavy pan and add the lemon grass, shallots, kaffir lime leaves, chilli, fish sauce and lime juice. Mix well. Cover the pan tightly and steam the mussels over a high heat, shaking the pan occasionally, for 5–7 minutes, until the shells have opened.

3 Using a slotted spoon, transfer the cooked mussels to a warmed serving dish or individual bowls. Discard any mussels that have failed to open.

4 Garnish the mussels with the thinly sliced spring onions and coriander leaves. Serve immediately.

Energy 26kcal/112kJ; Protein 4.5g; Carbohydrate 1g, of which sugars 0.8g; Fat 0.5g, of which saturates 0.1g, of which polyunsaturates 0.2g; Cholesterol 10mg; Calcium 52mg; Fibre 0.1g; Sodium 231mg.

MUSSELS AND CLAMS WITH LEMON GRASS AND COCONUT MILK ★

LEMON GRASS HAS AN INCOMPARABLE AROMATIC FLAVOUR AND IS WIDELY USED WITH ALL KINDS OF SEAFOOD IN THAILAND AS THE FLAVOURS MARRY SO PERFECTLY.

SERVES SIX

INGREDIENTS
900g/2lb fresh mussels
225g/8oz baby clams
120ml/4fl oz/½ cup dry white wine
1 bunch spring onions
   (scallions), chopped
1 lemon grass stalk, chopped
3 kaffir lime leaves, chopped
10ml/2 tsp Thai green curry paste
120ml/4fl oz/½ cup reduced-fat
   coconut milk
30ml/2 tbsp chopped fresh
   coriander (cilantro)
salt and ground black pepper
garlic chives, to garnish

1 Clean the mussels by pulling off the beards, scrubbing the shells well and scraping off any barnacles with the blade of a knife. Scrub the clams. Discard any mussels or clams that are damaged or broken or which do not close immediately when tapped sharply.

2 Put the wine in a large pan with the spring onions, lemon grass and lime leaves. Stir in the curry paste. Simmer until the wine has almost evaporated.

COOK'S TIPS
• In these days of marine pollution, it is unwise to gather fresh shellfish yourself. Those available from fish stores have either been farmed or have undergone a purging process to clean them.
• Depending on where you live, you may have difficulty obtaining clams. If so, use a few extra mussels instead.

3 Add the mussels and clams to the pan and increase the heat to high. Cover tightly and steam the shellfish for 5–6 minutes, until they open.

4 Using a slotted spoon, transfer the mussels and clams to a heated serving bowl, cover and keep hot. Discard any shellfish that remain closed. Strain the cooking liquid into a clean pan through a sieve lined with muslin (cheesecloth) and simmer briefly to reduce to about 250ml/8fl oz/1 cup.

5 Stir the coconut milk and chopped coriander into the sauce and season with salt and pepper to taste. Heat through. Pour the sauce over the mussels and clams, garnish with the garlic chives and serve immediately.

Energy 73kcal/309kJ; Protein 10.5g; Carbohydrate 2.1g, of which sugars 1.8g; Fat 1.2g, of which saturates 0.2g, of which polyunsaturates 0.4g; Cholesterol 26mg; Calcium 129mg; Fibre 0.7g; Sodium 271mg.

SPRING ROLLS WITH MUSHROOMS AND PORK ★

ONE OF THE MOST POPULAR FOODS THROUGHOUT VIETNAM IS THE SPRING ROLL, WHICH MAKES AN IDEAL QUICK SNACK. EVEN THOUGH THE SPRING ROLLS ARE DEEP FRIED, THE BRIEF COOKING TIME AND CAREFUL DRAINING ON KITCHEN PAPER MEANS THEY ARE VERY LOW IN FAT.

MAKES ABOUT 30

INGREDIENTS
30 dried rice wrappers
sunflower oil, for deep-frying
1 bunch fresh mint, stalks removed,
and *nuoc cham*, to serve
For the filling
50g/2oz dried bean thread
(cellophane) noodles, soaked in
warm water for 20 minutes
25g/1oz dried cloud ear (wood ear)
mushrooms, soaked in warm water
for 15 minutes
2 eggs
30ml/2 tbsp *nuoc mam*
2 garlic cloves, crushed
10ml/2 tsp sugar
1 onion, finely chopped
3 spring onions (scallions),
finely sliced
350g/12oz/1½ cups minced (ground)
lean pork
175g/6oz/1¾ cups cooked crab meat
or raw prawns (shrimp)
salt and ground black pepper

1 To make the filling, squeeze dry the soaked noodles and chop them into small pieces. Squeeze dry the soaked dried cloud ear mushrooms and chop them.

2 Beat the eggs in a bowl. Stir in the *nuoc mam*, garlic and sugar. Add the onion, spring onions, noodles, mushrooms, pork and crab meat or prawns. Season well with salt and ground black pepper.

COOK'S TIP
These spring rolls filled with rice noodles and served with fresh mint and *nuoc cham* are typically Vietnamese. You can substitute beansprouts for the noodles to create rolls more akin to the traditional version. Fresh mint leaves give these rolls a refreshing bite, but fresh coriander (cilantro), basil or flat leaf parsley will work just as well and give an interesting flavour. Dipped into a piquant sauce of your choice, the rolls are very moreish.

3 Have ready a damp dish towel, some clear film (plastic wrap) and a bowl of water. Dip a rice wrapper in the water and place it on the damp towel. Spoon about 15ml/1 tbsp of the spring roll filling on to the side nearest to you, just in from the edge. Fold the nearest edge over the filling, fold over the sides, tucking them in neatly, and then roll the whole wrapper into a tight cylinder. Place the roll on a plate and cover with clear film to keep it moist. Continue making spring rolls in the same way, using the remaining wrappers and filling.

4 Heat the sunflower oil in a wok or heavy pan for deep-frying. Make sure it is hot enough by dropping in a small piece of bread; it should foam and sizzle. Cook the spring rolls in batches, turning them in the oil so that they become golden all over. Drain them on kitchen paper and serve immediately with mint leaves to wrap around them and *nuoc cham* for dipping.

Energy 55kcal/232kJ; Protein 4.5g; Carbohydrate 7g, of which sugars 0.4g; Fat 0.9g, of which saturates 0.3g, of which polyunsaturates 0.1g; Cholesterol 31mg; Calcium 10mg; Fibre 0.1g; Sodium 24mg.

GRILLED PRAWNS WITH LEMON GRASS ★

*NEXT TO EVERY FISH STALL IN EVERY MARKET THERE IS BOUND TO BE SOMEONE COOKING UP
FRAGRANT, CITRUS-SCENTED SNACKS FOR YOU TO EAT AS YOU WANDER AROUND THE MARKET.
THE AROMATIC SCENT OF LEMON GRASS IS HARD TO RESIST.*

SERVES FOUR

INGREDIENTS
  16 king prawns (jumbo shrimp),
    cleaned, with shells intact
  120ml/4fl oz/½ cup *nuoc mam*
  30ml/2 tbsp sugar
  15ml/1 tbsp sunflower oil
  3 lemon grass stalks, trimmed and
    finely chopped

1 Using a small sharp knife, carefully slice open each king prawn shell along the back and pull out the black vein, using the point of the knife. Try to keep the rest of the shell intact. Place the deveined prawns in a shallow dish and set aside.

2 Put the *nuoc mam* in a small bowl with the sugar, and beat together until the sugar has dissolved completely. Add the oil and lemon grass and mix well.

COOK'S TIP
Big, juicy king prawns are best for this recipe, but you can use smaller ones if the large king prawns are not available.

3 Pour the marinade over the prawns, using your fingers to rub it all over the prawns and inside the shells too. Cover the dish with clear film (plastic wrap) and chill for at least 4 hours.

4 Cook the prawns on a barbecue or under a conventional grill (broiler) for 2–3 minutes each side. Serve with little bowls of water for rinsing sticky fingers.

Energy 97kcal/409kJ; Protein 9.2g; Carbohydrate 8.8g, of which sugars 8.7g; Fat 3.1g, of which saturates 0.4g, of which polyunsaturates 1.8g; Cholesterol 98mg; Calcium 46mg; Fibre 0g; Sodium 897mg.

POPIAH ★

HERE IS THE MALAYSIAN VERSION OF THE SPRING ROLL. DO NOT BE PUT OFF BY THE NUMBER OF
INGREDIENTS; IT TAKES A LITTLE TIME TO GET EVERYTHING TOGETHER BUT ONCE IT IS ALL ON THE
TABLE THE COOK CAN RETIRE AS GUESTS ASSEMBLE THEIR OWN.

MAKES ABOUT TWENTY-FOUR PANCAKES

INGREDIENTS
40g/1¹/₂oz/¹/₃ cup cornflour
(cornstarch)
215g/7¹/₂oz/generous 1³/₄ cups
plain (all-purpose) flour
salt
450ml/³/₄ pint/scant 2 cups water
6 eggs, beaten
spray sunflower oil, for frying
For the cooked filling
15ml/1 tbsp sunflower oil
1 onion, finely chopped
2 garlic cloves, crushed
115g/4oz cooked lean pork, chopped
115g/4oz crab meat or peeled
cooked prawns (shrimp), thawed
if frozen
115g/4oz drained canned bamboo
shoot, thinly sliced
1 small yam bean, peeled and grated
or 12 drained canned water
chestnuts, finely chopped
15–30ml/1–2 tbsp yellow
salted beans
15ml/1 tbsp light soy sauce
ground black pepper
For the fresh fillings
2 hard-boiled eggs, chopped
2 Chinese sausages, steamed
and sliced
115g/4oz packet fried tofu, each
piece halved
225g/8oz/4 cups beansprouts
115g/4oz crab meat or peeled
cooked prawns (shrimp)
¹/₂ cucumber, cut into matchsticks
small bunch of spring onions
(scallions), finely chopped
20 lettuce leaves, rinsed and dried
fresh coriander (cilantro) sprigs,
to garnish
selection of sauces, including bottled
chopped chillies, bottled chopped
garlic and hoisin sauce, to serve

COOK'S TIP
Yam beans are large tubers with a mild
sweet texture similar to water chestnuts.

1 Sift the flours and salt into a bowl.
Add the measured water and eggs and
mix to a smooth batter.

2 Spray a heavy non-stick frying pan
with sunflower oil, then pour in just
enough batter to cover the base.

3 As soon as it sets, flip and cook the
other side. The pancakes should be
quite thin. Repeat with the remaining
batter to make 20–24 pancakes in all.
Pile the cooked pancakes on top of
each other, with a layer of baking
parchment between each to prevent
them sticking. Wrap in foil and keep
warm in a low oven.

4 Make the cooked filling for the
popiah. Heat the oil in a wok and
stir-fry the onion and garlic together
for 5 minutes until softened but not
browned. Add the pork, crab meat or
prawns, bamboo shoot and grated
yam bean or water chestnuts. Stir-fry
the mixture over a medium heat for
2–3 minutes.

5 Add the salted yellow beans and
soy sauce to the wok, with pepper to
taste. Cover and cook the beans gently
for 15–20 minutes, adding a little
boiling water if the mixture starts to
dry out. Spoon into a serving bowl and
allow to cool.

6 Meanwhile, arrange the chopped
hard-boiled eggs, sliced Chinese
sausages, sliced tofu, beansprouts,
crab meat or prawns, cucumber
matchsticks, finely chopped spring
onions and lettuce leaves in piles on
a large platter or in separate bowls.
Spoon the bottled chopped chillies,
bottled chopped garlic and hoisin into
small bowls.

7 To serve, arrange the popiah on
a large warm platter. Each person
makes up his or her own popiah
by spreading a very small amount of
chopped chilli, garlic or hoisin sauce
on a pancake, adding a lettuce leaf,
a little of the cooked filling and a
small selection of the fresh ingredients.
The pancake wrapper should not be
over-filled.

8 The ends can be tucked in and the
pancake rolled up in typical spring roll
fashion, then eaten in the hand. They
also look attractive simply rolled with
the filling showing. The popiah can be
filled and rolled before guests arrive,
in which case, garnish with sprigs of
coriander. It is more fun though for
everyone to fill and roll their own.

Energy 94kcal/396kJ; Protein 6.7g; Carbohydrate 10g, of which sugars 0.7g; Fat 3.4g, of which saturates 0.8g, of which polyunsaturates 0.8g; Cholesterol 88mg; Calcium 60mg; Fibre 0.6g; Sodium 109mg.

CRUNCHY SUMMER ROLLS ★

THESE DELIGHTFUL RICE PAPER ROLLS FILLED WITH CRUNCHY RAW SUMMER VEGETABLES AND FRESH MINT AND CORIANDER ARE LIGHT AND REFRESHING, EITHER AS A SNACK OR AN APPETIZER TO A MEAL, AND ARE ENJOYED ALL OVER VIETNAM AND CAMBODIA.

SERVES FOUR

INGREDIENTS
12 round rice papers
1 lettuce, leaves separated and
    ribs removed
2–3 carrots, cut into julienne strips
1 small cucumber, peeled, halved
    lengthways and seeded, and cut
    into julienne strips
3 spring onions (scallions), trimmed
    and cut into julienne strips
225g/8oz mung beansprouts
1 bunch fresh mint leaves
1 bunch coriander (cilantro) leaves
dipping sauce, to serve
    (see Cook's Tips)

1 Pour some lukewarm water into a shallow dish. Soak the rice papers, 2–3 at a time, for about 5 minutes until they are pliable. Place the soaked papers on a clean dish towel and cover with a second dish towel to keep them moist.

2 Work with one paper at a time. Place a lettuce leaf towards the edge nearest to you, leaving about 2.5cm/1in to fold over. Place a mixture of the vegetables on top, followed by some mint and coriander leaves.

3 Fold the edge nearest to you over the filling, tuck in the sides, and roll tightly to the edge on the far side. Place the filled roll on a plate and cover with clear film (plastic wrap), so it doesn't dry out. Repeat with the remaining rice papers and vegetables. Serve with a dipping sauce of your choice. If you are making these summer rolls ahead of time, keep them in the refrigerator under a damp dish towel, so that they remain moist.

COOK'S TIPS
• In Vietnam, these crunchy filled rolls are often served with a light peanut dipping sauce. In Cambodia, they are accompanied by a dipping sauce called *tuk trey* (also the name of the national fish sauce), which is similar to the Vietnamese dipping sauce, *nuoc cham*, except that it has chopped peanuts in it. They are, in fact, delicious with any dipping sauce.
• Rice papers can be bought in Chinese and South-east Asian markets.

VARIATION
This recipe only uses vegetables, which are cut into equal lengths, but you can also add pre-cooked shredded lean chicken, pork or prawns (shrimp) to summer rolls.

Energy 107kcal/447kJ; Protein 3.9g; Carbohydrate 20.6g, of which sugars 4.4g; Fat 0.9g, of which saturates 0.1g, of which polyunsaturates 0.3g; Cholesterol 0mg; Calcium 62mg; Fibre 2.9g; Sodium 16mg.

CRISPY SPRING ROLLS ★

IT IS SAID THAT THESE FAMOUS SNACKS WERE TRADITIONALLY SERVED WITH TEA WHEN VISITORS CAME TO CALL AFTER THE NEW YEAR. AS THIS WAS SPRINGTIME, THEY CAME TO BE KNOWN AS SPRING ROLLS. BUY FRESH OR FROZEN SPRING ROLL WRAPPERS FROM ASIAN STORES.

MAKES TWELVE

INGREDIENTS
12 spring roll wrappers, thawed
   if frozen
30ml/2 tbsp plain (all-purpose) flour
   mixed to a paste with water
For the filling
   6 Chinese dried mushrooms,
      soaked for 30 minutes in
      warm water
   150g/5oz fresh firm tofu
   15ml/1 tbsp sunflower oil
   225g/8oz finely minced (ground)
      lean pork
   225g/8oz peeled cooked prawns
      (shrimp), roughly chopped
   2.5ml/¹/₂ tsp cornflour (cornstarch),
      mixed to a paste with 15ml/1 tbsp
      light soy sauce
   75g/3oz each shredded bamboo shoot
      or grated carrot, sliced water
      chestnuts and beansprouts
   6 spring onions (scallions) or 1 young
      leek, finely chopped
   2.5ml/¹/₂ tsp sesame oil
For the dipping sauce
   100ml/3¹/₂ fl oz/scant ¹/₂ cup
      light soy sauce
   15ml/1 tbsp chilli sauce or finely
      chopped fresh red chilli
   a little sesame oil
   rice vinegar, to taste

1 Make the filling. Drain the mushrooms. Cut off and discard the stems and slice the caps finely. Cut the tofu into slices of a similar size.

2 Heat the oil in a wok and stir-fry the pork for 2–3 minutes or until the colour changes. Add the prawns, cornflour paste and bamboo shoot or carrot. Stir in the water chestnuts.

COOK'S TIP
Thaw frozen spring roll wrappers at room temperature. Separate with a metal spatula. Cover with a damp cloth until needed.

3 Increase the heat, add the beansprouts and finely chopped spring onions or leek and toss the mixture for 1 minute. Stir in the dried Chinese mushrooms and tofu.

4 Off the heat, season the mixture to taste, and then stir in the sesame oil. Cool quickly on a large platter.

5 Separate the spring roll wrappers (see Cook's Tip). Place a wrapper on the work surface with one corner nearest you. Spoon some of the filling near the centre of the wrapper and fold the nearest corner over the filling. Smear a little of the flour paste on the free sides, turn the sides to the middle and roll up. Repeat this procedure with the remaining wrappers and filling.

6 Preheat the oven to 200°C/400°F/ Gas 6. Prepare a non-stick baking sheet or line a baking sheet with non-stick baking parchment. Lightly whisk the egg white with the oil and 5ml/1 tsp water. Generously brush the spring rolls with egg white, so they are moistened all over, and place on the baking sheet. Bake for about 20 minutes, until crisp and golden.

Energy 83kcal/349kJ; Protein 9.5g; Carbohydrate 7.9g, of which sugars 1.4g; Fat 1.7g, of which saturates 0.4g, of which polyunsaturates 0.5g; Cholesterol 48mg; Calcium 97mg; Fibre 0.5g; Sodium 645mg.

THAI SPRING ROLLS ★

CRUNCHY SPRING ROLLS ARE A POPULAR SNACK IN THAILAND. THAIS FILL THEIR VERSION WITH A
DELICIOUS GARLIC, PORK AND NOODLE MIXTURE.

MAKES ABOUT TWENTY-FOUR

INGREDIENTS
    24 × 15cm/6in square spring
        roll wrappers
    30ml/2 tbsp plain (all-purpose) flour
    1 egg white
    5ml/1 tsp sunflower oil
    Thai sweet chilli dipping sauce,
        to serve (optional)
For the filling
    4–6 Chinese dried mushrooms,
        soaked for 30 minutes in warm
        water to cover
    50g/2oz cellophane noodles
    15ml/1 tbsp sunflower oil
    2 garlic cloves, chopped
    2 fresh red chillies, seeded
        and chopped
    225g/8oz minced (ground) lean pork
    50g/2oz peeled cooked prawns
        (shrimp), thawed if frozen
    30ml/2 tbsp Thai fish sauce
    5ml/1 tsp sugar
    1 carrot, grated
    50g/2oz drained canned bamboo
        shoots, chopped
    50g/2oz/1 cup beansprouts
    2 spring onions, finely chopped
    15ml/1 tbsp chopped fresh
        coriander (cilantro)
    ground black pepper

1 Drain the mushrooms. Cut off the stems and discard; chop the caps finely.

2 Place the noodles in a large bowl, cover with boiling water and soak for 10 minutes. Drain the noodles and snip them into 5cm/2in lengths.

3 Heat the oil in a wok, add the garlic and chillies and stir-fry for 30 seconds. Transfer to a plate, add the pork and cook, stirring, until it has browned and is cooked through.

4 Add the noodles, mushrooms and prawns to the wok. Stir in the Thai fish sauce and sugar, then add ground black pepper to taste.

5 Tip the noodle mixture into a bowl and stir in the grated carrot, chopped bamboo shoots, beansprouts, finely chopped spring onions and chopped coriander together with the reserved chilli and pork mixture.

COOK'S TIP
Thai fish sauce or *nam pla* is one of the most important ingredients in Thai cuisine. It is made from fish, usually anchovies, which are salted, then fermented in wooden barrels to create the thin liquid that is the basis of the sauce. The strong flavour becomes less pronounced with cooking, and does not necessarily impart a fishy flavour to the dish.

6 Unwrap the spring roll wrappers. Cover them with a dampened dish towel while you are making the rolls, so that they do not dry out. Put the flour in a small bowl and stir in a little water to make a paste. Place a spoonful of filling in the centre of a spring roll wrapper.

7 Turn the bottom edge over to cover the filling, then fold in the left and right sides. Roll the wrapper up almost to the top edge then brush the top edge with the flour paste and seal. Fill the remaining wrappers in the same way, thinning the paste with a little water if it is too thick.

8 Preheat the oven to 220°C/425°F/ Gas 7. Prepare a non-stick baking sheet or line a baking sheet with baking parchment. Lightly whisk the egg white with the sunflower oil and 5ml/1 tsp water. Brush the spring rolls generously with egg white, so that they are moistened all over, and place on the baking tray. Bake for about 10 minutes, until lightly browned and crisp. Serve hot with Thai sweet chilli sauce, if you like.

Energy 46kcal/193kJ; Protein 3.3g; Carbohydrate 6.9g, of which sugars 0.7g; Fat 0.6g, of which saturates 0.2g, of which polyunsaturates 0.2g; Cholesterol 10mg; Calcium 17mg; Fibre 0.4g; Sodium 15mg.

LEMON GRASS SNAILS *

THE LIVE SNAILS SOLD IN VIETNAMESE MARKETS ARE USUALLY DESTINED FOR THIS POPULAR DELICACY.
SERVED STRAIGHT FROM THE BAMBOO STEAMER, THESE LEMON GRASS-INFUSED MORSELS ARE SERVED AS
AN APPETIZER, OR AS A SPECIAL SNACK, DIPPED IN NUOC CHAM.

SERVES FOUR

INGREDIENTS
  12 fresh snails in their shells
  115g/4oz lean minced (ground) pork,
    passed through the mincer twice
  2 lemon grass stalks, trimmed
    and finely chopped or ground
    (reserve the outer leaves)
  1 spring onion (scallions),
    finely chopped
  15g/½oz fresh root ginger, peeled
    and finely grated
  1 red Thai chilli, seeded and
    finely chopped
  5ml/1 tsp sesame oil
  sea salt and ground black pepper
  nuoc cham or other sauce,
    for dipping

2 Chop the snails finely and put them in a bowl. Add the minced pork, lemon grass, spring onions, ginger, chilli and oil. Season with salt and pepper and mix all the ingredients together.

4 Using your fingers, stuff each shell with the snail and pork mixture, gently pushing it between the lemon grass ends to the back of the shell so that it fills the shell completely.

1 Pull the snails out of their shells and place them in a colander. Rinse the snails thoroughly in plenty of cold water and pat dry with kitchen paper. Rinse the shells and leave to drain.

3 Select the best of the lemon grass leaves and tear each one into thin ribbons, roughly 7.5cm/3in long. Bend each ribbon in half and put it inside a snail shell, so that the ends are poking out. The idea is that each diner pulls the ends of the lemon grass ribbon to gently prize the steamed morsel out of its shell.

COOK'S TIP
Freshwater snails in their shells are available in South-east Asian markets, and some supermarkets and delicatessens. The idea of eating snails may have come from the French, who colonized Vietnam and Cambodia in the 19th and 20th centuries, but the method of cooking them in Vietnam is very different. Snails are plucked live from the water, straight into the bamboo steamer. If you ask for snails in a Vietnamese restaurant, they are likely to be cooked this way.

5 Fill a wok or large pan a third of the way up with water and bring it to the boil. Arrange the snail shells, open side up, in a steamer that fits the wok or pan.

6 Place the lid on the steamer and steam for about 10 minutes, until the mixture is cooked. Serve hot with *nuoc cham* or another strong-flavoured dipping sauce of your choice, such as soy sauce spiked with chopped chillies.

Energy 85kcal/357kJ; Protein 12g; Carbohydrate 0.4g, of which sugars 0.4g; Fat 4g, of which saturates 1.2g, of which polyunsaturates 0.9g; Cholesterol 36mg; Calcium 29mg; Fibre 0.7g; Sodium 38mg.

VEGETARIAN MAIN DISHES

Combined with nuts and tofu in moderation, vegetarian dishes
provide a healthy basis for many delicious meals. The wide
range of different vegetables, together with herbs, spices and
sauces, makes Asian cooking a real pleasure for vegetarians
trying to cut down on fat and cholesterol in their diet.
An added attraction is that most dishes are very quick and
easy to make. Aromatic vegetable curries, unusual stir-fries,
stuffed vegetables and a warming stew are included here.

TOFU AND VEGETABLE THAI CURRY ★★

TRADITIONAL THAI INGREDIENTS — CHILLIES, GALANGAL, LEMON GRASS AND KAFFIR LIME LEAVES — GIVE THIS CURRY A WONDERFULLY FRAGRANT AROMA. THE TOFU NEEDS TO MARINATE FOR AT LEAST 2 HOURS, SO BEAR THIS IN MIND WHEN TIMING YOUR MEAL.

SERVES FOUR

INGREDIENTS
  175g/6oz firm tofu
  45ml/3 tbsp dark soy sauce
  5ml/1 tsp sesame oil
  5ml/1 tsp chilli sauce
  2.5cm/1in piece fresh root ginger,
    peeled and finely grated
  1 head broccoli, about 225g/8oz
  ½ head cauliflower, about 225g/8oz
  15ml/1 tbsp sunflower oil
  1 onion, sliced
  200ml/7fl oz/scant 1 cup reduced-fat
    coconut milk
  350ml/12fl oz/1½ cups water
  1 red (bell) pepper, seeded
    and chopped
  175g/6oz/generous 1 cup green
    beans, halved
  115g/4oz/1½ cups shiitake or button
    (white) mushrooms, halved
  shredded spring onions (scallions),
    to garnish
  boiled jasmine rice or noodles,
    to serve
For the curry paste
  2 fresh red or green chillies, seeded
    and chopped
  1 lemon grass stalk, chopped
  2.5cm/1in piece fresh
    galangal, chopped
  2 kaffir lime leaves
  10ml/2 tsp ground coriander
  a few fresh coriander (cilantro)
    sprigs, including the stalks
  45ml/3 tbsp water

1 Rinse and drain the tofu. Using a sharp knife, cut it into 2.5cm/1in cubes. Place the cubes in the base of an ovenproof dish in a single layer.

2 Mix together the soy sauce, sesame oil, chilli sauce and grated ginger in a jug (pitcher) and pour over the tofu. Toss gently to coat all the cubes evenly, cover with clear film (plastic wrap) and leave to marinate for at least 2 hours or overnight if possible, turning and basting the tofu occasionally.

3 Make the curry paste. Place the chillies, lemon grass, galangal, lime leaves, ground coriander and fresh coriander in a food processor and process until well blended. Add the water and process to a thick paste.

4 Preheat the oven to 190°C/375°F/ Gas 5. Cut the broccoli and cauliflower into small florets. Cut any stalks into thin slices.

5 Heat the sunflower oil in a frying pan and add the sliced onion. Cook over a low heat for about 8 minutes, until soft and lightly browned. Stir in the curry paste and the coconut milk. Add the water and bring to the boil.

6 Stir in the red pepper, green beans, broccoli and cauliflower. Transfer to a Chinese sand pot or earthenware casserole. Cover and place towards the bottom of the oven.

7 Stir the tofu and marinade, then place the dish on a shelf near the top of the oven. Cook for 30 minutes. Remove both the dish and the sand pot or casserole from the oven. Add the tofu, with any remaining marinade, to the curry, with the mushrooms, and stir well.

8 Return the sand pot or casserole to the oven, reduce the temperature to 180°C/350°F/Gas 4 and cook for about 15 minutes, or until the vegetables are tender. Garnish with the spring onions and serve with the rice or noodles.

COOK'S TIP
Tofu or beancurd is made from soya beans and is sold in blocks. It is a creamy white colour and naturally low in fat. Tofu has a bland flavour and its absorbent nature means that it takes on the flavours of marinades or other foods with which it is cooked.

Energy 155kcal/646kJ; Protein 10.9g; Carbohydrate 12.2g, of which sugars 10.5g; Fat 7.2g, of which saturates 1.1g, of which polyunsaturates 3.8g; Cholesterol 0mg; Calcium 333mg; Fibre 5.3g; Sodium 875mg.

SWEET AND SOUR VEGETABLES WITH TOFU ★

BIG, BOLD AND BEAUTIFUL, THIS IS A HEARTY STIR-FRY THAT WILL SATISFY THE HUNGRIEST GUESTS. IT IS PACKED WITH COLOURFUL VEGETABLES INCLUDING CORN COBS, RED PEPPERS AND GREEN MANGETOUTS.

SERVES FOUR

INGREDIENTS

4 shallots
3 garlic cloves
15ml/1 tbsp sunflower oil
250g/9oz Chinese leaves (Chinese
 cabbage), shredded
8 baby corn cobs, sliced on
 the diagonal
2 red (bell) peppers, seeded and
 thinly sliced
200g/7oz/1¾ cups mangetouts
 (snow peas), trimmed and sliced
250g/9oz tofu, rinsed, drained and
 cut in 1cm/½in cubes
60ml/4 tbsp vegetable stock
30ml/2 tbsp light soy sauce
15ml/1 tbsp granulated sugar
30ml/2 tbsp rice vinegar
2.5ml/½ tsp dried chilli flakes
small bunch coriander
 (cilantro), chopped

1 Slice the shallots thinly using a sharp knife. Finely chop the garlic.

2 Heat the oil in a wok or large frying pan and cook the shallots and garlic for 2–3 minutes over a medium heat, until golden. Do not let the garlic burn or it will taste bitter.

3 Add the shredded cabbage, toss over the heat for 30 seconds, then add the corn cobs and repeat the process.

4 Add the red peppers, mangetouts and tofu in the same way, each time adding a single ingredient and tossing it over the heat for about 30 seconds before adding the next ingredient.

5 Pour in the stock and soy sauce. Mix together the sugar and vinegar in a small bowl, stirring until the sugar has dissolved, then add to the wok or pan. Sprinkle over the chilli flakes and coriander, toss to mix well and serve.

Energy 144kcal/604kJ; Protein 5.2g; Carbohydrate 23.7g, of which sugars 18.2g; Fat 3.7g, of which saturates 0.5g, of which polyunsaturates 2.2g; Cholesterol 0mg; Calcium 73mg; Fibre 4.7g; Sodium 611mg.

SPICY TOFU WITH BASIL AND PEANUTS ★★

AROMATIC PEPPER LEAVES ARE OFTEN USED AS THE HERB ELEMENT IN THAILAND BUT, BECAUSE THESE ARE QUITE DIFFICULT TO FIND OUTSIDE SOUTH-EAST ASIA, YOU CAN USE BASIL LEAVES INSTEAD.

SERVES FOUR

INGREDIENTS

    3 lemon grass stalks, finely chopped
    45ml/3 tbsp soy sauce
    2 red Serrano chillies, seeded and
        finely chopped
    2 garlic cloves, crushed
    5ml/1 tsp ground turmeric
    10ml/2 tsp sugar
    300g/11oz tofu, rinsed, drained,
        patted dry and cut into
        bitesize cubes
    15ml/1 tbsp sunflower oil
    15ml/1 tbsp roasted peanuts,
        chopped
    1 bunch fresh basil, stalks removed
    salt

1 In a bowl, mix together the lemon grass, soy sauce, chillies, garlic, turmeric and sugar until the sugar has dissolved. Add a little salt to taste and add the tofu, making sure it is well coated. Leave to marinate for 1 hour.

VARIATION
Replace the fresh basil with kaffir lime leaves, coriander (cilantro) leaves or curry leaves, all of which would work well in this simple stir-fry.

2 Heat a wok or heavy pan. Pour in the oil, add the marinated tofu, and cook, stirring frequently, until it is golden brown on all sides. Add the peanuts and most of the basil leaves.

3 Divide the marinated tofu and peanut mixture among individual serving dishes. Then sprinkle the remaining basil leaves over the top and serve hot or at room temperature.

Energy 115kcal/480kJ; Protein 7.4g; Carbohydrate 4.5g, of which sugars 3.9g; Fat 7.6g, of which saturates 1g, of which polyunsaturates 3.7g; Cholesterol 0mg; Calcium 388mg; Fibre 0.2g; Sodium 804mg.

THAT VEGETABLE CURRY WITH LEMON GRASS RICE ★

FRAGRANT JASMINE RICE, SUBTLY FLAVOURED WITH LEMON GRASS AND CARDAMOM, IS THE PERFECT ACCOMPANIMENT FOR THIS RICHLY SPICED VEGETABLE CURRY.

SERVES FOUR

INGREDIENTS
10ml/2 tsp sunflower oil
200ml/7fl oz/scant 1 cup reduced-fat
    coconut milk
550ml/18fl oz/2½ cups
    vegetable stock
225g/8oz new potatoes, halved or
    quartered, if large
8 baby corn cobs
5ml/1 tsp golden caster
    (superfine) sugar
185g/6½oz/1¼ cups broccoli florets
1 red (bell) pepper, seeded and
    sliced lengthways
115g/4oz spinach, tough stalks
    removed, leaves shredded
30ml/2 tbsp chopped fresh
    coriander (cilantro)
salt and ground black pepper
For the spice paste
1 fresh red chilli, seeded
    and chopped
3 fresh green chillies, seeded
    and chopped
1 lemon grass stalk, outer leaves
    removed and lower 5cm/2in
    finely chopped
2 shallots, chopped
finely grated rind of 1 lime
2 garlic cloves, chopped
5ml/1 tsp ground coriander
2.5ml/½ tsp ground cumin
1cm/½in piece fresh galangal,
    finely chopped, or 2.5ml/½ tsp
    dried galangal (optional)
30ml/2 tbsp chopped fresh
    coriander (cilantro)
15ml/1 tbsp chopped fresh
    coriander (cilantro) roots and
    stems (optional)
For the rice
225g/8oz/1¼ cups jasmine
    rice, rinsed
6 cardamom pods, bruised
1 lemon grass stalk, outer leaves
    removed, cut into 3 pieces
475ml/16fl oz/2 cups water

1 Make the spice paste. Place all the ingredients in a food processor and process to a coarse paste. Heat the oil in a large, heavy pan. Add the paste and stir-fry over a medium heat for 1–2 minutes, until fragrant.

2 Pour in the coconut milk and stock and bring to the boil. Reduce the heat, add the potatoes and simmer gently for about 15 minutes, until almost tender.

3 Meanwhile, put the rice into a large pan with the cardamoms and lemon grass. Pour in the water. Bring to the boil, reduce the heat, cover, and cook for 10–15 minutes, until the water has been absorbed and the rice is tender.

4 When the rice is cooked and slightly sticky, season to taste with salt, then replace the lid and leave to stand for about 10 minutes.

5 Add the baby corn to the potatoes, season with salt and pepper to taste, then cook for 2 minutes. Stir in the sugar, broccoli and red pepper, and cook for 2 minutes more, or until the vegetables are tender.

6 Stir the shredded spinach and half the fresh coriander into the vegetable mixture. Cook for 2 minutes, then spoon the curry into a warmed serving dish.

7 Remove and discard the cardamom pods and lemon grass from the rice and fluff up the grains with a fork. Garnish the curry with the remaining fresh coriander and serve with the rice.

COOK'S TIP
Cardamom pods may be dark brown, cream, or pale green. The brown pods are usually larger, coarser and do not have such a good flavour as the others. Always remove them before serving.

Energy 313kcal/1313kJ; Protein 9.8g; Carbohydrate 61.4g, of which sugars 7.7g; Fat 3.2g, of which saturates 0.5g, of which polyunsaturates 1.5g; Cholesterol 0mg; Calcium 134mg; Fibre 4.1g; Sodium 439mg.

VEGETABLE FOREST CURRY ★

THIS IS A THIN, SOUPY CURRY WITH LOTS OF FRESH GREEN VEGETABLES AND ROBUST FLAVOURS.
IN THE FORESTED REGIONS OF THAILAND, WHERE IT ORIGINATED, IT WOULD BE MADE USING EDIBLE
WILD LEAVES AND ROOTS. SERVE IT WITH RICE OR NOODLES FOR A SIMPLE LUNCH OR SUPPER.

SERVES TWO

INGREDIENTS
600ml/1 pint/2½ cups water
5ml/1 tsp Thai vegetarian red
  curry paste
5cm/2in piece fresh galangal or fresh
  root ginger
90g/3½oz/scant 1 cup green beans
2 kaffir lime leaves, torn
8 baby corn cobs, halved widthways
2 heads Chinese broccoli, chopped
90g/3½oz/generous
  3 cups beansprouts
15ml/1 tbsp drained bottled green
  peppercorns, crushed
10ml/2 tsp granulated sugar
5ml/1 tsp salt

1 Heat the water in a large pan. Add
the red curry paste and stir until it has
dissolved completely. Bring to the boil.

2 Meanwhile, using a sharp knife,
peel and finely chop the fresh galangal
or root ginger.

3 Add the galangal or ginger, green
beans, lime leaves, baby corn cobs,
broccoli and beansprouts to the pan.
Stir in the crushed peppercorns, sugar
and salt. Bring back to the boil, then
reduce the heat to low and simmer for
2 minutes. Serve immediately.

Energy 154kcal/643kJ; Protein 14.9g; Carbohydrate 14.1g, of which sugars 11.8g; Fat 4.5g, of which saturates 0.8g, of which polyunsaturates 2.4g; Cholesterol 0mg; Calcium 173mg; Fibre 9.1g; Sodium 678mg.

JUNGLE CURRY ★

VARIATIONS OF THIS FIERY, FLAVOURSOME VEGETARIAN CURRY CAN BE FOUND ALL OVER SOUTHERN VIETNAM. A FAVOURITE WITH THE BUDDHIST MONKS AND OFTEN SOLD FROM COUNTRYSIDE STALLS, IT CAN BE SERVED WITH PLAIN RICE OR NOODLES, OR CHUNKS OF CRUSTY BREAD.

SERVES FOUR

INGREDIENTS

15ml/1 tbsp sunflower oil
2 onions, roughly chopped
2 lemon grass stalks, roughly
  chopped and bruised
4 green Thai chillies, seeded and
  finely sliced
4cm/1½in galangal or fresh root
  ginger, peeled and chopped
3 carrots, peeled, halved lengthways
  and sliced
115g/4oz long beans
grated rind of 1 lime
10ml/2 tsp soy sauce
15ml/1 tbsp rice vinegar
5ml/1 tsp black peppercorns,
  crushed
15ml/1 tbsp sugar
10ml/2 tsp ground turmeric
115g/4oz canned bamboo shoots
75g/3oz spinach, steamed and
  roughly chopped
150ml/¼ pint/⅔ cup reduced-fat
  coconut milk
salt
chopped fresh coriander (cilantro)
  and mint leaves, to garnish

COOK'S TIPS
• Also known as yard-long beans or asparagus beans, snake beans are eaten all over South-east Asia. They may grow up to 40cm/16in long and can be found in Asian stores. There are two common varieties, pale green and darker green, the latter have the better flavour. When buying, choose young, narrow specimens with under-developed seeds, as these will be the most tender. They do not have strings, and preparation is simply trimming and chopping them into short lengths. As they mature, snake beans can become quite tough. They should be used before they turn yellow.
• Jungle curry should be fiery, almost dominated by the chilli. In Vietnam it is often eaten for breakfast or a great pick-me-up at any time of day.

1 Heat a wok or heavy pan and add the oil. Once hot, stir in the onions, lemon grass, chillies and galangal or ginger. Add the carrots and beans with the lime rind and stir-fry for 1–2 minutes.

2 Add the soy sauce and rice vinegar to the wok and stir well. Add the crushed peppercorns, sugar and turmeric, then stir in the bamboo shoots and the chopped spinach.

3 Stir in the coconut milk and simmer for about 10 minutes, until the vegetables are tender. Season with salt, and serve hot, garnished with fresh coriander and mint.

Energy 119kcal/496kJ; Protein 3.8g; Carbohydrate 18.6g, of which sugars 15.3g; Fat 3.8g, of which saturates 0.5g, of which polyunsaturates 2.2g; Cholesterol 0mg; Calcium 125mg; Fibre 4.3g; Sodium 60mg.

AUBERGINE AND SWEET POTATO STEW WITH COCONUT MILK ★

SCENTED WITH FRAGRANT LEMON GRASS, GINGER AND LOTS OF GARLIC, THIS IS A PARTICULARLY GOOD COMBINATION OF FLAVOURS. AUBERGINES AND SWEET POTATOES GO WELL TOGETHER AND THE COCONUT MILK ADDS A MELLOW NOTE.

SERVES SIX

INGREDIENTS

400g/14oz baby aubergines
   (eggplant) or 2 standard aubergines
15ml/1 tbsp sunflower oil
225g/8oz Thai red shallots or other
   small shallots or pickling onions
5ml/1 tsp fennel seeds,
   lightly crushed
4–5 garlic cloves, thinly sliced
25ml/1½ tbsp finely chopped fresh
   root ginger
475ml/16fl oz/2 cups vegetable stock
2 lemon grass stalks, outer layers
   discarded, finely chopped
   or minced
15g/½oz/⅔ cup fresh coriander
   (cilantro), stalks and leaves
   chopped separately
3 kaffir lime leaves, lightly bruised
2–3 small fresh red chillies
45ml/3 tbsp Thai green curry paste
675g/1½lb sweet potatoes, peeled
   and cut into thick chunks
400ml/14fl oz/1⅔ cups reduced-fat
   coconut milk
2.5–5ml/½–1 tsp palm sugar
250g/9oz/3½ cups mushrooms,
   thickly sliced
juice of 1 lime, to taste
salt and ground black pepper
boiled rice and 18 fresh Thai basil
   or ordinary basil leaves, to serve

2 Heat half the oil in a wide pan or deep, lidded frying pan. Add the aubergines and cook (uncovered) over a medium heat, stirring occasionally, until lightly browned on all sides. Remove from the pan and set aside.

3 Slice 4–5 of the shallots. Cook the whole shallots in the oil remaining in the pan, until lightly browned. Set aside with the aubergines. Add the remaining oil to the pan and cook the sliced shallots, fennel seeds, garlic and ginger over a low heat for 5 minutes.

4 Pour in the vegetable stock, then add the lemon grass, chopped coriander stalks and any roots, lime leaves and whole chillies. Cover and simmer over a low heat for 5 minutes.

5 Stir in 30ml/2 tbsp of the curry paste and the sweet potatoes. Simmer gently for about 10 minutes, then return the aubergines and browned shallots to the pan and cook for a further 5 minutes.

6 Stir in the coconut milk and the sugar. Season to taste with salt and pepper, then stir in the mushrooms and simmer gently for 5 minutes, or until all the vegetables are cooked and tender.

7 Stir in the remaining curry paste and lime juice to taste, followed by the chopped coriander leaves. Adjust the seasoning and ladle the vegetables into warmed bowls. Sprinkle basil leaves over the stew and serve with rice.

COOK'S TIP
Although this is called a stew, green curry paste is an important ingredient, as it is in most of these recipes. The quantity given is only a guide, however, so use less if you prefer.

1 Trim the aubergines. Slice baby aubergines in half lengthways. Cut standard aubergines into chunks.

Energy 147kcal/627kJ; Protein 3.2g; Carbohydrate 29.1g, of which sugars 11.3g; Fat 3g, of which saturates 0.6g, of which polyunsaturates 1.5g; Cholesterol 0mg; Calcium 72mg; Fibre 4.9g; Sodium 125mg.

FISH AND SHELLFISH

Fish is a main source of protein in the Thai diet, which is hardly
surprising considering the vast lengths of coastline. Oily fish
contains Omega-3 fatty acids that help lower cholesterol and reduce
blood pressure. Fish is steamed, stir-fried, baked, grilled with
local spices or herbs, and served in curries and sauces. Serving a
fish whole, rather than cutting it into portions, has great appeal
in Asia. Impress your guests with Stir-fried Baby Squid with
Ginger, Hot and Fragrant Trout or Spicy Pan-seared Tuna.

SINIGANG ★

MANY FILIPINOS WOULD CONSIDER THIS SOURED HEALTHY SOUP-LIKE STEW TO BE THEIR NATIONAL DISH. IT IS ALWAYS SERVED WITH NOODLES OR RICE. IN ADDITION, FISH — IN THE FORM OF EITHER PRAWNS OR THIN SLIVERS OF FISH FILLET — IS OFTEN ADDED FOR GOOD MEASURE.

3 Pour the prepared fish stock into a large pan and add the diced mooli. Cook the mooli for 5 minutes, then add the beans and continue to cook for 3–5 minutes more.

SERVES SIX

INGREDIENTS

   15ml/1 tbsp tamarind pulp
   150ml/¼ pint/⅔ cup warm water
   2 tomatoes
   115g/4oz spinach or Chinese leaves
    (Chinese cabbage)
   115g/4oz peeled cooked large prawns
    (shrimp), thawed if frozen
   1.2 litres/2 pints/5 cups prepared
    fish stock (see Cook's Tip)
   ½ mooli (daikon), peeled and diced
   115g/4oz green beans, cut into
    1cm/½in lengths
   225g/8oz piece of cod or haddock
    fillet, skinned and cut into strips
   Thai fish sauce, to taste
   squeeze of lemon juice, to taste
   salt and ground black pepper
   boiled rice or noodles, to serve

1 Put the tamarind pulp in a bowl and pour over the warm water. Set aside while you peel and chop the tomatoes, discarding the seeds. Strip the spinach or Chinese leaves from the stems and tear into small pieces.

2 Remove the heads and shells from the prawns, leaving the tails intact.

4 Add the fish strips, tomato and spinach. Strain in the tamarind juice and cook for 2 minutes. Stir in the prawns and cook for 1–2 minutes to heat. Season with salt and pepper and add a little fish sauce and lemon juice to taste. Transfer to individual serving bowls and serve immediately, with rice or noodles.

COOK'S TIP

A good fish stock is essential for this dish. Ask your fishmonger for about 675g/1½lb fish bones. Wash them, then place in a large pan with 2 litres/ 3½ pints/8 cups water. Add half a peeled onion, a piece of bruised peeled ginger, and a little salt and pepper. Bring to the boil, skim, then simmer for 20 minutes. Cool slightly, then strain. Freeze unused fish stock.

Energy 52kcal/218kJ; Protein 10.6g; Carbohydrate 1.3g, of which sugars 1.3g; Fat 0.5g, of which saturates 0.1g, of which polyunsaturates 0.2g; Cholesterol 55mg; Calcium 31mg; Fibre 0.6g; Sodium 62mg.

STIR-FRIED PRAWNS <u>WITH</u> TAMARIND ★

THE SOUR, TANGY FLAVOUR THAT IS CHARACTERISTIC OF MANY THAI DISHES COMES FROM TAMARIND.
FRESH TAMARIND PODS FROM THE TAMARIND TREE CAN SOMETIMES BE BOUGHT, BUT PREPARING THEM
FOR COOKING IS A LABORIOUS PROCESS. IT IS MUCH EASIER TO USE A BLOCK OF TAMARIND PASTE.

SERVES FOUR TO SIX

INGREDIENTS
  6 dried red chillies
  15ml/1 tbsp sunflower oil
  30ml/2 tbsp chopped onion
  30ml/2 tbsp palm sugar or light
    muscovado (brown) sugar
  30ml/2 tbsp water
  15ml/1 tbsp Thai fish sauce
  90ml/6 tbsp tamarind juice, made
    by mixing tamarind paste with
    warm water
  450g/1lb raw prawns
    (shrimp), peeled
  15ml/1 tbsp fried chopped garlic
  30ml/2 tbsp fried sliced shallots
  2 spring onions (scallions), chopped,
    to garnish

1 Heat a wok or large frying pan, but do not add any oil at this stage. Add the dried chillies and dry-fry them by pressing them against the surface of the wok or pan with a spatula, turning them occasionally. Do not let them burn. Set them aside to cool slightly.

2 Add the oil to the wok or pan and reheat. Add the chopped onion and cook over a medium heat, stirring occasionally, for 2–3 minutes, until softened and golden brown.

3 Add the sugar, water, fish sauce, dry-fried red chillies and the tamarind juice, stirring constantly until the sugar has dissolved. Bring to the boil, then lower the heat slightly.

4 Add the prawns, garlic and shallots. Toss over the heat for 3–4 minutes, until the prawns are cooked. Garnish with the spring onions and serve.

COOK'S TIP
Leave a few prawns in their shells for a garnish, if you like.

Energy 100kcal/422kJ; Protein 13.6g; Carbohydrate 6.6g, of which sugars 6g; Fat 2.3g, of which saturates 0.3g, of which polyunsaturates 1.3g; Cholesterol 146mg; Calcium 65mg; Fibre 0.3g; Sodium 321mg.

CURRIED SEAFOOD WITH COCONUT MILK ★

THIS CURRY IS BASED ON A THAI CLASSIC. THE LOVELY GREEN COLOUR IS IMPARTED BY THE FINELY CHOPPED CHILLI AND FRESH HERBS ADDED DURING THE LAST FEW MOMENTS OF COOKING.

SERVES FOUR

INGREDIENTS
225g/8oz small ready-prepared squid
225g/8oz raw tiger prawns
(jumbo shrimp)
400ml/14fl oz/1⅔ cups reduced-fat
coconut milk
2 kaffir lime leaves, finely shredded
30ml/2 tbsp Thai fish sauce
450g/1lb firm white fish fillets,
skinned, boned and cut into chunks
2 fresh green chillies, seeded and
finely chopped
30ml/2 tbsp torn fresh basil or
coriander (cilantro) leaves
squeeze of fresh lime juice
cooked Thai jasmine rice, to serve
For the curry paste
6 spring onions (scallions),
coarsely chopped
4 fresh coriander (cilantro) stems,
coarsely chopped, plus 45ml/3 tbsp
chopped fresh coriander (cilantro)
4 kaffir lime leaves, shredded
8 fresh green chillies, seeded and
coarsely chopped
1 lemon grass stalk,
coarsely chopped
2.5cm/1in piece fresh root ginger,
peeled and coarsely chopped
45ml/3 tbsp chopped fresh basil
5ml/1 tsp sunflower oil

1 Make the curry paste. Put all the ingredients, except the oil, in a food processor and process to a paste. Alternatively, pound together in a mortar with a pestle. Stir in the oil.

2 Rinse the squid and pat dry with kitchen paper. Cut the bodies into rings and halve the tentacles, if necessary.

3 Heat a wok until hot, add the prawns and stir-fry, without any oil, for about 4 minutes, until they turn pink.

4 Remove the prawns from the wok and leave to cool slightly, then peel off the shells, saving a few with shells on for the garnish. Make a slit along the back of each one and remove the black vein.

5 Pour the coconut milk into the wok, then bring to the boil over a medium heat, stirring constantly. Add 30ml/ 2 tbsp of curry paste, the shredded lime leaves and fish sauce and stir well to mix. Reduce the heat to low and simmer gently for about 10 minutes.

6 Add the squid, prawns and chunks of fish and cook for about 2 minutes, until the seafood is tender. Take care not to overcook the squid as it will become tough very quickly.

7 Just before serving, stir in the chillies and the torn basil or coriander leaves. Taste and adjust the flavour with a squeeze of lime juice. Garnish the curry with prawns in their shells, and serve with Thai jasmine rice.

VARIATIONS
• You can use any firm-fleshed white fish for this curry, such as monkfish, cod, haddock or John Dory.
• If you prefer, you could substitute shelled scallops for the squid. Slice them in half horizontally and add them with the prawns (shrimp). As with the squid, be careful not to overcook them.

Energy 211kcal/894kJ; Protein 39.8g; Carbohydrate 5.9g, of which sugars 5.2g; Fat 3.3g, of which saturates 0.7g, of which polyunsaturates 1.2g; Cholesterol 288mg; Calcium 116mg; Fibre 0.6g; Sodium 351mg.

STIR-FRIED SCALLOPS AND PRAWNS ★

SERVE THIS LIGHT, DELICATE DISH FOR LUNCH OR SUPPER ACCOMPANIED BY AROMATIC STEAMED RICE OR FINE RICE NOODLES AND STIR-FRIED PAK CHOI. THIS COMBINATION OF FRESH SEAFOOD AND LIGHTLY COOKED VEGETABLES PRODUCES A DISH THAT IS HIGH IN FLAVOUR AND LOW IN FAT.

SERVES FOUR

INGREDIENTS

15ml/1 tbsp sunflower oil
500g/1¼lb raw tiger prawns
  (shrimp), peeled
1 star anise
225g/8oz scallops, halved if large
2.5cm/1in piece fresh root ginger,
  peeled and grated
2 garlic cloves, thinly sliced
1 red (bell) pepper, seeded and cut
  into thin strips
115g/4oz/1¾ cups shiitake or button
  (white) mushrooms, thinly sliced
juice of 1 lemon
5ml/1 tsp cornflour (cornstarch)
30ml/2 tbsp light soy sauce
chopped fresh chives,
  to garnish
salt and ground black pepper

1 Heat the oil in a wok until very hot. Put in the prawns and star anise and stir-fry over a high heat for 2 minutes. Add the scallops, ginger and garlic and stir-fry for 1 minute more, by which time the prawns should have turned pink and the scallops should be opaque. Season with a little salt and plenty of pepper and then remove from the wok using a slotted spoon. Discard the star anise.

2 Add the red pepper and mushrooms to the wok and stir-fry for 1–2 minutes.

3 Make a cornflour paste by combining the cornflour with 30ml/2 tbsp cold water. Stir until smooth.

4 Pour the lemon juice, cornflour paste and soy sauce into the wok, bring to the boil and bubble for 1–2 minutes, stirring all the time, until the sauce is smooth and slightly thickened.

VARIATIONS
Other types of shellfish can be used in this dish. Try it with thinly sliced rings of squid, or use mussels or clams. You could even substitute bitesize chunks of firm white fish, such as monkfish, cod or haddock, for the scallops. These can be added to the dish in step 1, as with the scallops.

Energy 212kcal/892kJ; Protein 36.2g; Carbohydrate 6.6g, of which sugars 3.3g; Fat 4.6g, of which saturates 0.8g, of which polyunsaturates 2.3g; Cholesterol 270mg; Calcium 122mg; Fibre 1g; Sodium 877mg.

STEAMED MUSSELS WITH CHILLI AND GINGER ★

THIS SIMPLE DISH IS VIETNAM'S VERSION OF THE FRENCH CLASSIC, MOULES MARINIÈRE. THE VIETNAMESE STEAM THE MUSSELS OPEN IN A HERB-INFUSED STOCK RATHER THAN IN WHITE WINE. LEMON GRASS AND CHILLI FLAVOUR THE DISH INSTEAD OF WINE AND PARSLEY.

SERVES FOUR

INGREDIENTS
600ml/1 pint/2½ cups chicken stock
1 Thai chilli, seeded and chopped
2 shallots, finely chopped
3 lemon grass stalks,
  finely chopped
1 bunch ginger or basil leaves
1kg/2¼lb fresh mussels, cleaned
  and bearded
salt and ground black pepper

COOK'S TIP
Aromatic ginger leaves are hard to find outside Asia. If you can't find them, basil or coriander (cilantro) will work well.

1 Pour the chicken stock into a deep pan. Add the chopped chilli, shallots, lemon grass and most of the ginger or basil leaves, retaining a few leaves for the garnish. Bring to the boil. Cover and simmer for 10–15 minutes, then season to taste.

2 Discard any mussels that remain open when tapped, then add the remaining mussels to the stock. Stir well, cover and cook for 2 minutes, or until the mussels have opened. Discard any that remain closed. Ladle the mussels and cooking liquid into individual bowls.

Energy 75kcal/318kJ; Protein 13.6g; Carbohydrate 1.5g, of which sugars 1.1g; Fat 1.7g, of which saturates 0.3g, of which polyunsaturates 0.5g; Cholesterol 30mg; Calcium 176mg; Fibre 0.8g; Sodium 162mg.

PRAWN AND CAULIFLOWER CURRY ★

THIS IS A BASIC FISHERMAN'S CURRY FROM THE SOUTHERN COAST OF VIETNAM. SIMPLE TO MAKE, IT WOULD USUALLY BE EATEN FROM A COMMUNAL BOWL, OR FROM THE WOK ITSELF, AND SERVED WITH NOODLES, RICE OR CHUNKS OF BAGUETTE TO MOP UP THE DELICIOUSLY FRAGRANT SAUCE.

SERVES FOUR

INGREDIENTS
    450g/1lb raw tiger prawns (jumbo
        shrimp), shelled and cleaned
    juice of 1 lime
    15ml/1 tbsp sunflower oil
    1 red onion, roughly chopped
    2 garlic cloves, roughly chopped
    2 Thai chillies, seeded and chopped
    1 cauliflower, broken into florets
    5ml/1 tsp sugar
    2 star anise, dry-fried and ground
    10ml/2 tsp fenugreek, dry-fried
        and ground
    450ml/¾ pint/2 cups reduced-fat
        coconut milk
    chopped fresh coriander (cilantro)
        leaves, to garnish
    salt and ground black pepper

1 In a bowl, toss the prawns in the lime juice and set aside. Heat a wok or heavy pan and add the oil. Stir in the onion, garlic and chillies. As they brown, add the cauliflower. Stir-fry for 2–3 minutes.

VARIATION
Other popular combinations include prawns with butternut squash or pumpkin.

2 Toss in the sugar and spices. Add the coconut milk, stirring to make sure it is thoroughly combined. Reduce the heat and simmer for 10–15 minutes, or until the liquid has reduced and thickened a little. Add the prawns and lime juice and cook for 1–2 minutes, or until the prawns turn opaque. Season to taste, and sprinkle with coriander. Serve hot.

Energy 157kcal/664kJ; Protein 24.7g; Carbohydrate 10.4g, of which sugars 9.4g; Fat 2.2g, of which saturates 0.6g, of which polyunsaturates 0.7g; Cholesterol 219mg; Calcium 169mg; Fibre 2.7g; Sodium 352mg.

LOBSTER AND CRAB STEAMED IN BEER ★

IN SPITE OF ITS APPEARANCE ON MENUS IN RESTAURANTS THAT SPECIALIZE IN THE COMPLEX AND REFINED IMPERIAL DISHES OF VIETNAM, THIS RECIPE IS VERY EASY TO MAKE. IT MAY BE EXPENSIVE, BUT IT'S A WONDERFUL DISH FOR A SPECIAL OCCASION.

SERVES FOUR TO SIX

INGREDIENTS
    4 uncooked lobsters, about
      450g/1lb each
    4 uncooked crabs, about
      225g/8oz each
    600ml/1 pint/2½ cups beer
    4 spring onions (scallions), trimmed
      and chopped into long pieces
    4cm/1½ in fresh root ginger, peeled
      and finely sliced
    2 green or red Thai chillies, seeded
      and finely sliced
    3 lemon grass stalks, finely sliced
    1 bunch fresh dill, fronds chopped
    1 bunch each fresh basil and
      coriander (cilantro), stalks removed,
      leaves chopped
    about 30ml/2 tbsp *nuoc mam*, plus
      extra for serving
    juice of 1 lemon
    salt and ground black pepper

1 Clean the lobsters and crabs thoroughly and rub them with salt and pepper. Place them in a large steamer and pour the beer into the base.

2 Sprinkle half the spring onions, ginger, chillies, lemon grass and herbs over the lobsters and crabs, and steam for about 10 minutes, or until the lobsters turn red. Lift them on to a warmed serving dish.

VARIATIONS
Prawns (shrimp) and mussels are also delicious cooked this way. Replace the lemon with lime if you like.

3 Add the remaining flavouring ingredients to the beer with the *nuoc mam* and lemon juice. Pour into a dipping bowl and serve immediately with the hot lobsters and crabs, with extra splashes of *nuoc mam*, if you like.

COOK'S TIP
Whether you cook the lobsters and crabs at the same time depends on the number of people you are cooking for and the size of your steamer. However, they don't take long to cook so it is easy to steam them in batches. In the markets and restaurants of Vietnam, you can find crabs that are 60cm/24in in diameter, which may feed several people but require a huge steamer. Depending on the size and availability of the lobsters and crabs, you can make this recipe for as many people as you like, because the quantities are simple to adjust. For those who like their food fiery, splash a little chilli sauce into the beer broth.

Energy 190kcal/801kJ; Protein 35.2g; Carbohydrate 1.5g, of which sugars 1.4g; Fat 4.9g, of which saturates 0.7g, of which polyunsaturates 1.6g; Cholesterol 158mg; Calcium 86mg; Fibre 0.8g; Sodium 589mg.

NORTHERN FISH CURRY ★★

THIS IS A THIN, SOUPY CURRY WITH WONDERFULLY STRONG FLAVOURS. SERVE IT IN BOWLS WITH LOTS OF STICKY RICE TO SOAK UP THE DELICIOUS JUICES.

SERVES FOUR

INGREDIENTS
    350g/12oz salmon fillet
    500ml/17fl oz/2¼ cups
      vegetable stock
    4 shallots, finely chopped
    2 garlic cloves, finely chopped
    2.5cm/1in piece fresh galangal,
      finely chopped
    1 lemon grass stalk, finely chopped
    2.5ml/½ tsp dried chilli flakes
    15ml/1 tbsp Thai fish sauce
    5ml/1 tsp palm sugar or light
      muscovado (brown) sugar

1 Place the salmon in the freezer for 30–40 minutes to firm up the flesh slightly. Remove and discard the skin, then use a sharp knife to cut the fish into 2.5cm/1in cubes, removing any stray bones with your fingers or with tweezers as you do so.

2 Pour the stock into a large, heavy pan and bring it to the boil over a medium heat. Add the shallots, garlic, galangal, lemon grass, chilli flakes, fish sauce and sugar. Bring back to the boil, stir well, then reduce the heat and simmer gently for 15 minutes.

3 Add the fish, bring back to the boil, then turn off the heat. Leave the curry to stand for 10–15 minutes until the fish is cooked through, then serve.

Energy 172kcal/717kJ; Protein 18.2g; Carbohydrate 3.2g, of which sugars 2.5g; Fat 9.7g, of which saturates 1.7g, of which polyunsaturates 2.7g; Cholesterol 44mg; Calcium 24mg; Fibre 0.3g; Sodium 307mg.

ESCABECHE ★

THIS PICKLED FISH DISH IS EATEN WHEREVER THERE ARE — OR HAVE BEEN — SPANISH SETTLERS.
IT IS ESPECIALLY POPULAR IN THE PHILIPPINES WHERE IT IS SERVED WITH BOILED OR STEAMED RICE.

SERVES SIX

INGREDIENTS
675–900g/1¹/₂–2lb white fish fillets,
  such as sole or plaice
45–60ml/3–4 tbsp seasoned flour
sunflower oil, for shallow frying
For the sauce
2.5cm/1in piece fresh root ginger,
  peeled and thinly sliced
2–3 garlic cloves, crushed
1 onion, cut into thin rings
15ml/1 tbsp sunflower oil
¹/₂ large green (bell) pepper,
  seeded and cut in small
  neat squares
¹/₂ large red (bell) pepper, seeded
  and cut in small neat squares
1 carrot, cut into matchsticks
25ml/1¹/₂ tbsp cornflour (cornstarch)
450ml/³/₄ pint/scant 2 cups water
45–60ml/3–4 tbsp herb or
  cider vinegar
15ml/1 tbsp light soft brown sugar
5–10ml/1–2 tsp Thai fish sauce
salt and ground black pepper
1 small chilli, seeded and sliced
  and spring onions (scallions), finely
  shredded, to garnish (optional)
boiled rice, to serve

3 Make the sauce in a wok or large
frying pan. Fry the ginger, garlic and
onion in the oil for 5 minutes or until
the onion is softened but not browned.

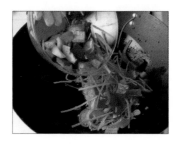

4 Add the pepper squares and carrot
strips and stir-fry for 1 minute.

5 Put the cornflour in a small bowl
and add a little of the water to make
a paste. Stir in the remaining water,
the vinegar and the sugar. Pour the
cornflour mixture over the vegetables in
the wok and stir until the sauce boils
and thickens a little. Season with fish
sauce and salt and pepper if needed.

6 Add the fish to the sauce and reheat
briefly without stirring. Transfer to a
warmed serving platter and garnish with
chilli and spring onions, if liked. Serve
with boiled rice.

COOK'S TIP
Red snapper or small sea bass could be
used for this recipe, in which case ask
your fishmonger to cut them into fillets.

1 Wipe the fish fillets and leave them
whole, or cut into serving portions, if
you like. Pat dry on kitchen paper then
dust lightly with seasoned flour.

2 Heat oil for shallow frying in a frying
pan and fry the fish in batches until
golden and almost cooked. Transfer to
an ovenproof dish and keep warm.

Energy 130kcal/550kJ; Protein 21.3g; Carbohydrate 9.3g, of which sugars 5.2g; Fat 1.1g, of which saturates 0.2g, of which polyunsaturates 0.4g; Cholesterol 52mg; Calcium 34mg; Fibre 1g; Sodium 74mg.

JUNGLE FISH COOKED IN BANANA LEAVES ★

STEAMING FRESHWATER FISH IN BANANA LEAVES OVER HOT CHARCOAL IS A TRADITIONAL METHOD OF COOKING IN THE JUNGLE. BANANA LEAVES ARE LARGE AND TOUGH, AND SERVE AS BASIC COOKING VESSELS AND WRAPPERS FOR ALL SORTS OF FISH AND MEAT.

SERVES FOUR

INGREDIENTS
  350g/12oz freshwater fish fillets,
    such as trout, cut into
    bitesize chunks
  6 banana leaves (see Cook's Tip)
  spray sunflower vegetable oil
  sticky rice, noodles or salad, to serve
For the marinade
  2 shallots
  5cm/2in turmeric root, peeled
    and grated
  2 spring onions (scallions),
    finely sliced
  2 garlic cloves, crushed
  1–2 green Thai chillies, seeded
    and finely chopped
  15ml/1 tbsp *nuoc mam*
  2.5ml/½ tsp raw cane sugar
  salt and ground black pepper

1 To make the marinade, grate the shallots into a bowl, then combine with the other marinade ingredients, Season with salt and pepper. Toss the chunks of fish in the marinade, then cover and chill for 6 hours, or overnight.

VARIATION
This dish can be made with any of the catfish or carp family, or even talapia.

2 Prepare a barbecue. Place one of the banana leaves on a flat surface and spray it with oil. Place the marinated fish on the banana leaf, spreading it out evenly, then fold over the sides to form an envelope. Place this envelope, fold side down, on top of another leaf and fold that one in the same manner. Repeat with the remaining leaves until they are all used up.

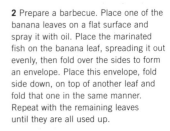

3 Secure the last layer of banana leaf with a piece of bendy wire. Place the banana leaf packet on the barbecue. Cook for about 20 minutes, turning it over from time to time to make sure it is cooked on both sides – the outer leaves will burn. Carefully untie the wire (it will be hot) and unravel the packet. Check that the fish is cooked and serve with sticky rice, noodles or salad.

COOK'S TIP
Banana leaves are available in some African and Asian stores and markets. If you can't find them, wrap the fish in vine leaves that have been soaked in cold water, or large flexible cabbage leaves. You can also use foil.

Energy 84kcal/352kJ; Protein 16.3g; Carbohydrate 1.5g, of which sugars 1.1g; Fat 1.4g, of which saturates 0.2g, of which polyunsaturates 0.8g; Cholesterol 40mg; Calcium 12mg; Fibre 0.2g; Sodium 320mg.

STEAMED FISH <u>WITH</u> CHILLI SAUCE ★

STEAMING IS ONE OF THE HEALTHIEST METHODS OF COOKING FISH. BY LEAVING THE FISH WHOLE AND ON THE BONE, MAXIMUM FLAVOUR IS RETAINED AND THE FLESH REMAINS BEAUTIFULLY MOIST. THE BANANA LEAF IS BOTH AUTHENTIC AND ATTRACTIVE, BUT YOU CAN USE BAKING PARCHMENT.

SERVES FOUR

INGREDIENTS

  1 large or 2 medium firm fish such
    as sea bass or grouper, scaled
    and cleaned
  30ml/2 tbsp rice wine
  3 fresh red chillies, seeded and
    thinly sliced
  2 garlic cloves, finely chopped
  2cm/¾ in piece fresh root ginger,
    peeled and finely shredded
  2 lemon grass stalks, crushed and
    finely chopped
  2 spring onions
    (scallions), chopped
  30ml/2 tbsp Thai fish sauce
  juice of 1 lime
  1 fresh banana leaf
For the chilli sauce
  10 fresh red chillies, seeded
    and chopped
  4 garlic cloves, chopped
  60ml/4 tbsp Thai fish sauce
  15ml/1 tbsp granulated sugar
  75ml/5 tbsp fresh lime juice

1 Thoroughly rinse the fish under cold running water. Pat it dry with kitchen paper. With a sharp knife, slash the skin of the fish a few times on both sides.

2 Mix together the rice wine, chillies, garlic, shredded ginger, lemon grass and spring onions in a non-metallic bowl. Add the fish sauce and lime juice and mix to a paste. Place the fish on the banana leaf and spread the spice paste evenly over it, rubbing it in well where the skin has been slashed.

3 Put a rack or a small upturned plate in the base of a wok. Pour in boiling water to a depth of 5cm/2in. Lift the banana leaf, together with the fish, and place it on the rack or plate. Cover with a lid and steam for 10–15 minutes, or until the fish is cooked.

4 Meanwhile, make the sauce. Place all the ingredients in a food processor and process until smooth. If the mixture seems to be too thick, add a little cold water. Scrape into a serving bowl.

5 Serve the fish hot, on the banana leaf if you like, with the sweet chilli sauce to spoon over the top.

Energy 147kcal/619kJ; Protein 28.4g; Carbohydrate 5.5g, of which sugars 5.3g; Fat 1.3g, of which saturates 0.2g, of which polyunsaturates 0.5g; Cholesterol 69mg; Calcium 56mg; Fibre 1g; Sodium 898mg.

FISH ᴵᴺ COCONUT CUSTARD ★★

This is a Khmer classic. Rich and sumptuous, amok trey crops up all over Cambodia. In Phnom Penh, there are restaurants that specialize in it. The fish is steamed in a custard, made with coconut milk and flavoured with the Cambodian herbal paste, kroeung.

SERVES FOUR

INGREDIENTS
  2 x 400ml/14oz cans reduced-fat
    coconut milk
  3 eggs
  80ml/3fl oz *kroeung*
  15ml/1 tbsp *tuk trey*
  10ml/2 tsp palm sugar or honey
  1 kg/2¼lb fresh, skinned white fish
    fillets, cut into 8 pieces
  1 small bunch chopped fresh
    coriander (cilantro), plus a few
    whole sprigs, to garnish
  jasmine rice or crusty bread and
    salad, to serve

VARIATION
This dish can also be cooked in the oven in a bain marie. Cook at 160°C/325°F/Gas 3 for about 50 minutes.

1 Half fill a wok or large pan with water. Set a bamboo or stainless-steel steamer over it and put the lid on. Bring the water to the boil.

2 In a bowl, beat the reduced-fat coconut milk with the eggs, *kroeung*, *tuk trey* and sugar or honey, until everything is well blended and the sugar has dissolved.

3 Place the fish fillets in a heatproof dish that will fit in the steamer. Pour the coconut mixture over the fish and place the dish in the steamer. Put the lid back on the steamer and reduce the heat so that the custard won't curdle. Steam over gently simmering water until the fish is cooked. Garnish with coriander and serve immediately with jasmine rice or crusty bread and salad.

Energy 314kcal/1324kJ; Protein 51.1g; Carbohydrate 13.6g, of which sugars 13.6g; Fat 6.5g, of which saturates 1.8g, of which polyunsaturates 1.2g; Cholesterol 258mg; Calcium 102mg; Fibre 0g; Sodium 423mg.

CATFISH COOKED <u>IN A</u> CLAY POT ★

WONDERFULLY EASY AND TASTY, THIS SOUTHERN-STYLE VIETNAMESE AND CAMBODIAN DISH IS A CLASSIC. IN THE SOUTH OF VIETNAM, CLAY POTS ARE REGULARLY USED FOR COOKING AND THEY ENHANCE BOTH THE LOOK AND TASTE OF THIS TRADITIONAL DISH.

SERVES FOUR

INGREDIENTS

30ml/2 tbsp sugar
15ml/1 tbsp sunflower oil
2 garlic cloves, crushed
45ml/3 tbsp *nuoc mam*
350g/12oz catfish fillets, cut
   diagonally into 2 or 3 pieces
4 spring onions (scallions), cut
   into bitesize pieces
ground black pepper
chopped fresh coriander (cilantro),
   to garnish
fresh bread, to serve

2 Stir the *nuoc mam* into the caramel mixture and add 120ml/4fl oz/¹/2 cup boiling water, then toss in the catfish pieces, making sure they are well coated with the sauce. Cover the pot, reduce the heat and simmer for about 5 minutes.

3 Remove the lid, season with ground black pepper and gently stir in the spring onions. Simmer for a further 3–4 minutes to thicken the sauce, garnish with fresh coriander, and serve immediately straight from the pot with chunks of fresh bread.

1 Place the sugar in a clay pot or heavy pan, and add 15ml/1 tbsp water to wet it. Heat the sugar until it begins to turn golden brown, then add the oil and crushed garlic.

Energy 128kcal/537kJ; Protein 16.4g; Carbohydrate 8.3g, of which sugars 8.3g; Fat 3.4g, of which saturates 0.4g, of which polyunsaturates 2g; Cholesterol 40mg; Calcium 18mg; Fibre 0.2g; Sodium 54mg.

CHICKEN
AND DUCK

Chicken is a low-fat meat and stars in an astonishing variety of Asian recipes — stir-fried with ginger or chillies, roasted with spices, or grilled, curried, or braised in coconut milk. This chapter contains classic curries, traditional Chicken Satay with Peanut Sauce, fruity Duck in a Spicy Orange Sauce and also some more unusual recipes — including Spicy Chicken with Young Ginger and Coriander — all specially adapted for the low-fat, low-cholesterol diet.

FRAGRANT RICE <u>WITH</u> CHICKEN, MINT <u>AND</u> NUOC CHAM ★

THIS REFRESHING DISH CAN BE SERVED SIMPLY, DRIZZLED WITH NUOC CHAM, OR AS PART OF A CELEBRATORY MEAL THAT MIGHT INCLUDE FISH OR CHICKEN, EITHER GRILLED OR ROASTED WHOLE, AND ACCOMPANIED BY PICKLES AND A TABLE SALAD.

2 Put the rice in a heavy pan and stir in the stock. When the rice settles, check that the stock sits roughly 2.5cm/1in above the rice; if not, top it up. Bring the liquid to the boil, cover the pan and cook for about 25 minutes, or until all the water has been absorbed.

SERVES FOUR

INGREDIENTS
  350g/12oz/1¾ cups long grain rice,
    rinsed and drained
  2–3 shallots, halved and finely sliced
  1 bunch of fresh mint, stalks
    removed, leaves finely shredded
  2 spring onions (scallions), finely
    sliced, to garnish
  nuoc cham, to serve
For the stock
  2 meaty chicken legs
  1 onion, peeled and quartered
  4cm/1½in fresh root ginger, peeled
    and coarsely chopped
  15ml/1 tbsp *nuoc mam*
  3 black peppercorns
  1 bunch of fresh mint
  sea salt

1 To make the stock, put the chicken legs into a deep pan. Add all the other ingredients, except the salt, and pour in 1 litre/1¾ pints/4 cups water. Bring the water to the boil, skim off any foam, then reduce the heat and simmer gently with the lid on for 1 hour. Remove the lid, increase the heat and simmer for a further 30 minutes to reduce the stock. Skim off any fat, strain the stock and season with salt. Measure 750ml/1¼ pints/3 cups stock. Remove the chicken meat from the bone and shred.

VARIATIONS
Any meat or fish can be added to this basic recipe. Try strips of stir-fried pork, slices of Chinese sausage or a handful of prawns (shrimp). Simply toss into the rice along with the shredded chicken.

3 Remove the pan from the heat and, using a fork, add the shredded chicken, shallots and most of the mint. Cover the pan again and leave the flavours to mingle for 10 minutes. Tip the rice into bowls, or on to a serving dish, garnish with the remaining mint and the spring onions, and serve with *nuoc cham*.

Energy 426kcal/1784kJ; Protein 25.6g; Carbohydrate 72.9g, of which sugars 1.8g; Fat 3.1g, of which saturates 0.7g, of which polyunsaturates 0.6g; Cholesterol 92mg; Calcium 53mg; Fibre 0.5g; Sodium 82mg.

SPICY CHICKEN WITH YOUNG GINGER AND CORIANDER ★★

GINGER PLAYS A BIG ROLE IN CAMBODIAN COOKING, PARTICULARLY IN THE STIR-FRIED DISHES. WHENEVER POSSIBLE, THE JUICIER AND MORE PUNGENT YOUNG GINGER IS USED. THIS IS A SIMPLE AND DELICIOUS WAY TO COOK CHICKEN, PORK OR BEEF.

SERVES FOUR

INGREDIENTS

15ml/1 tbsp sunflower oil
3 garlic cloves, finely sliced
    in strips
50g/2oz fresh young root ginger,
    finely sliced in strips
2 Thai chillies, seeded and finely
    sliced in strips
4 skinless chicken fillets or 4 boned
    chicken legs, skinned and cut
    into bitesize chunks
30ml/2 tbsp *tuk prahoc*
10ml/2 tsp sugar
1 small bunch coriander (cilantro)
    stalks removed, roughly chopped
ground black pepper
jasmine rice and crunchy salad or
    baguette, to serve

1 Heat a wok or heavy pan and add the oil. Add the garlic, ginger and chillies, and stir-fry until fragrant and golden. Add the chicken and toss it around the wok for 1–2 minutes.

COOK'S TIP
Young ginger is available in Chinese and South-east Asian markets.

2 Stir in the *tuk prahoc* and sugar, and stir-fry for a further 4–5 minutes until cooked. Season with pepper and add some of the fresh coriander. Transfer the chicken to a serving dish and garnish with the remaining coriander. Serve hot with jasmine rice and a crunchy salad with fresh herbs, or with chunks of freshly baked baguette.

Energy 187kcal/786kJ; Protein 27.5g; Carbohydrate 4g, of which sugars 3.8g; Fat 6.9g, of which saturates 1g, of which polyunsaturates 3.7g; Cholesterol 79mg; Calcium 35mg; Fibre 0.9g; Sodium 75mg.

RED CHICKEN CURRY <u>WITH</u> BAMBOO SHOOTS ★

BAMBOO SHOOTS HAVE A LOVELY CRUNCHY TEXTURE. IT IS QUITE ACCEPTABLE TO USE CANNED ONES, AS FRESH BAMBOO IS NOT READILY AVAILABLE IN THE WEST. BUY CANNED WHOLE BAMBOO SHOOTS, WHICH ARE CRISPER AND OF BETTER QUALITY THAN SLICED SHOOTS. RINSE BEFORE USING.

SERVES SIX

INGREDIENTS
475ml/16fl oz/2 cups reduced-fat
  coconut milk
450g/1lb skinless chicken fillets, cut
  into bitesize pieces
30ml/2 tbsp Thai fish sauce
15ml/1 tbsp sugar
475ml/16fl oz/2 cups
  chicken stock
225g/8oz drained canned bamboo
  shoots, rinsed and sliced
5 kaffir lime leaves, torn
chopped fresh red chillies and
  kaffir lime leaves, to garnish
For the red curry paste
5ml/1 tsp coriander seeds
2.5ml/½ tsp cumin seeds
12–15 fresh red chillies, seeded
  and roughly chopped
4 shallots, thinly sliced
2 garlic cloves, chopped
15ml/1 tbsp chopped galangal
2 lemon grass stalks, chopped
3 kaffir lime leaves, chopped
4 fresh coriander (cilantro) roots
10 black peppercorns
good pinch of ground cinnamon
5ml/1 tsp ground turmeric
2.5ml/½ tsp shrimp paste
5ml/1 tsp salt
15ml/1 tbsp sunflower oil

2 Add the oil, a little at a time, mixing or processing well after each addition. Transfer to a jar and keep in the refrigerator until ready to use.

3 Pour the coconut milk into a large heavy pan. Bring the milk to the boil, stirring constantly until it has separated.

1 Make the red curry paste. Dry-fry the coriander and cumin seeds for 1–2 minutes, then put in a mortar with the remaining ingredients except the oil and pound to a paste.

4 Stir in 30ml/2 tbsp of the red curry paste and cook the mixture for 2–3 minutes, stirring constantly. Remaining red curry paste can be kept in the refrigerator for up to 3 months.

5 Add the chicken fillets, Thai fish sauce and sugar to the pan. Stir well, then cook for 5–6 minutes until the chicken changes colour and is lightly golden and cooked through. Stir the chicken constantly to prevent the mixture from sticking to the bottom of the pan.

6 Pour the chicken stock into the pan, then add the sliced bamboo shoots and the torn kaffir lime leaves. Bring back to the boil over a medium heat, stirring constantly to prevent the chicken from sticking. Then remove the curry from the heat and season with salt and pepper to taste if necessary.

7 To serve, spoon the curry immediately into a warmed serving dish and garnish with chopped red chillies and kaffir lime leaves.

VARIATION
Instead of, or as well as, bamboo shoots, use straw mushrooms. These are available as dried mushrooms or in cans from Asian stores and supermarkets. Whether you are using dried or canned mushrooms, stir into the dish a few minutes before serving the curry.

COOK'S TIP
It is essential to use chicken breast fillets, rather than any other cut, for this curry, as it is cooked very quickly. Look out for diced chicken or strips of chicken (which are often labelled "stir-fry chicken") in the supermarket.

Energy 131kcal/552kJ; Protein 18.8g; Carbohydrate 7.5g, of which sugars 7.2g; Fat 3g, of which saturates 0.6g, of which polyunsaturates 1.3g; Cholesterol 55mg; Calcium 51mg; Fibre 0.5g; Sodium 153mg.

SOUTHERN CHICKEN CURRY ★★

A MILD COCONUT CURRY FLAVOURED WITH TURMERIC, CORIANDER AND CUMIN SEEDS THAT DEMONSTRATES THE INFLUENCE OF MALAYSIAN COOKING ON THAI CUISINE.

SERVES SIX

INGREDIENTS

30ml/2 tbsp sunflower oil
1 large garlic clove, crushed
1 chicken, weighing about 1.5kg/
  3–3½lb, chopped into
  12 large pieces
400ml/14fl oz/1⅔ cups reduced-fat
  coconut milk
250ml/8fl oz/1 cup chicken stock
30ml/2 tbsp Thai fish sauce
30ml/2 tbsp sugar
juice of 2 limes
To garnish
2 small fresh red chillies, seeded and
  finely chopped
1 bunch spring onions (scallions),
  thinly sliced
For the curry paste
5ml/1 tsp dried chilli flakes
2.5ml/½ tsp salt
5cm/2in piece fresh turmeric or
  5ml/1 tsp ground turmeric
2.5ml/½ tsp coriander seeds
2.5ml/½ tsp cumin seeds
5ml/1 tsp dried shrimp paste

1 First make the curry paste. Put all the ingredients in a mortar, food processor or spice grinder and pound, process or grind to a smooth paste.

2 Heat the oil in a wok or frying pan and cook the garlic until golden. Add the chicken and cook until golden. Remove the chicken and set aside.

3 Reheat the oil and add the curry paste and then half the coconut milk. Cook for a few minutes until fragrant.

4 Return the chicken to the wok or pan, add the stock, mixing well, then add the remaining coconut milk, the fish sauce, sugar and lime juice. Stir well and bring to the boil, then lower the heat and simmer for 15 minutes.

5 Turn the curry into six warm serving bowls and sprinkle with the chopped fresh chillies and spring onions to garnish. Serve immediately.

VARIATION
For a delicious curry that is even lower in fat, remove the skin before cooking the chicken in step 2.

COOK'S TIP
Use a large sharp knife or a Chinese cleaver to chop the chicken into pieces. Wash the board, knife and your hands thoroughly afterwards in hot, soapy water as chicken is notorious for harbouring harmful micro-organisms and bacteria.

Energy 222kcal/935kJ; Protein 29g; Carbohydrate 9.8g, of which sugars 9.5g; Fat 7.7g, of which saturates 1.7g, of which polyunsaturates 3.2g; Cholesterol 144mg; Calcium 50mg; Fibre 0.4g; Sodium 231mg.

CHICKEN AND LEMON GRASS CURRY ★

THIS FRAGRANT AND TRULY DELICIOUS CURRY IS EXCEPTIONALLY EASY AND TAKES LESS THAN TWENTY MINUTES TO PREPARE AND COOK — A PERFECT MID-WEEK MEAL.

SERVES FOUR

INGREDIENTS
10ml/2 tsp sunflower oil
2 garlic cloves, crushed
500g/1¼ lb skinless, boneless
  chicken thighs, chopped into
  small pieces
45ml/3 tbsp Thai fish sauce
120ml/4fl oz/½ cup
  chicken stock
5ml/1 tsp granulated sugar
1 lemon grass stalk, chopped into
  4 sticks and lightly crushed
5 kaffir lime leaves, rolled into
  cylinders and thinly sliced across,
  plus extra to garnish
chopped roasted peanuts
  and chopped fresh coriander
  (cilantro), to garnish
For the curry paste
1 lemon grass stalk,
  coarsely chopped
2.5cm/1in piece fresh galangal,
  peeled and coarsely chopped
2 kaffir lime leaves, chopped
3 shallots, coarsely chopped
6 coriander (cilantro) roots,
  coarsely chopped
2 garlic cloves
2 fresh green chillies, seeded and
  coarsely chopped
5ml/1 tsp shrimp paste
5ml/1 tsp ground turmeric

1 Make the curry paste. Place all the ingredients in a large mortar, or food processor and pound with a pestle or process to a smooth paste.

2 Heat the sunflower oil in a wok or large, heavy frying pan, add the garlic and cook over a low heat, stirring frequently, until golden brown. Be careful not to let the garlic burn or it will taste bitter. Add the curry paste and stir-fry with the garlic for about 30 seconds more.

3 Add the chicken pieces to the pan and stir until thoroughly coated with the curry paste. Stir in the Thai fish sauce and chicken stock, with the sugar, and cook, stirring constantly, for 2 minutes more.

4 Add the lemon grass and lime leaves, reduce the heat and simmer for 10 minutes. If the mixture begins to dry out, add a little more stock or water.

5 Remove the lemon grass, if you like. Spoon the curry into four dishes, garnish with the lime leaves, peanuts and coriander and serve immediately.

Energy 122kcal/512kJ; Protein 17.4g; Carbohydrate 3.7g, of which sugars 3g; Fat 4.3g, of which saturates 0.8g, of which polyunsaturates 1.6g; Cholesterol 85mg; Calcium 77mg; Fibre 1.6g; Sodium 131mg.

MEAT
DISHES

Meat curries are traditional in many South-east Asian
countries, but they contain relatively small amounts of meat
and plenty of vegetables, rice and noodles, making them an
excellent choice for anyone trying to cut down on red meat.
Stir-frying is another popular way of cooking meat, a technique
that has the advantage of combining speed with a minimum of
fat. Try some of these delicious recipes for a quick and healthy
supper, including Lemon Grass Pork and Thai Beef Salad.

PORK <u>ON</u> LEMON GRASS STICKS ★

THIS SIMPLE RECIPE MAKES A SUBSTANTIAL SNACK, AND THE LEMON GRASS STICKS NOT ONLY ADD A SUBTLE FLAVOUR BUT ALSO MAKE A GOOD TALKING POINT.

SERVES FOUR

INGREDIENTS

   300g/11oz minced (ground)
     lean pork
   4 garlic cloves, crushed
   4 fresh coriander (cilantro) roots,
     finely chopped
   2.5ml/½ tsp granulated sugar
   15ml/1 tbsp soy sauce
   salt and ground black pepper
   8 x 10cm/4in lengths of lemon
     grass stalk
   sweet chilli sauce, to serve

VARIATION

Slimmer versions of these pork sticks are perfect for parties. The mixture will be enough for 12 lemon grass sticks if you use it sparingly.

1 Place the minced pork, crushed garlic, chopped coriander root, sugar and soy sauce in a large bowl. Season with salt and pepper to taste and mix well.

2 Divide into eight portions and mould each one into a ball. It may help to dampen your hands before shaping the mixture to prevent it from sticking.

3 Stick a length of lemon grass halfway into each ball, then press the meat mixture around the lemon grass to make a shape like a chicken leg.

4 Cook the pork sticks under a hot grill (broiler) for 3–4 minutes on each side, until golden and cooked through. Serve with the chilli sauce for dipping.

Energy 111kcal/467kJ; Protein 17.5g; Carbohydrate 3.3g, of which sugars 1.4g; Fat 3.2g, of which saturates 1.1g, of which polyunsaturates 0.6g; Cholesterol 47mg; Calcium 29mg; Fibre 1g; Sodium 323mg.

LAMB SATÉ ★

THESE TASTY LAMB SKEWERS ARE TRADITIONALLY SERVED WITH DAINTY DIAMOND-SHAPED PIECES OF COMPRESSED RICE, WHICH ARE SURPRISINGLY SIMPLE TO MAKE. OFFER THE REMAINING SAUCE FOR DIPPING.

MAKES THIRTY SKEWERS

INGREDIENTS
  1kg/2¼lb leg of lamb, boned
  3 garlic cloves, crushed
  15–30ml/1–2 tbsp chilli sambal or
    5–10ml/1–2 tsp chilli powder
  90ml/6 tbsp dark soy sauce
  juice of 1 lemon
  salt and ground black pepper
  spray sunflower oil, for spraying
For the chilli sauce
  6 garlic cloves, crushed
  15ml/1 tbsp chilli sambal or
    2–3 fresh chillies, seeded and
    ground to a paste
  90ml/6 tbsp dark soy sauce
  25ml/1½ tbsp lemon juice
  30ml/2 tbsp boiling water
To serve
  thinly sliced onion
  cucumber wedges (optional)
  compressed-rice shapes (see
    Cook's Tip)

1 Cut the lamb into neat 1cm/½in cubes. Remove any pieces of gristle, and trim off any excess fat. Spread out the lamb cubes in a single layer in a shallow bowl.

2 Put the garlic, chilli sambal or chilli powder, soy sauce and lemon juice in a mortar. Add salt and pepper and grind to a paste. Alternatively, process the mixture using a food processor. Pour over the lamb and mix to coat. Cover and leave in a cool place for at least 1 hour. Soak wooden or bamboo skewers in water to prevent them from scorching during cooking.

3 Prepare the chilli sauce. Put the crushed garlic into a bowl. Add the chilli sambal or fresh chillies, soy sauce, lemon juice and boiling water. Stir well. Preheat the grill.

4 Thread the meat on to the skewers. Spray the skewered meat with oil and grill, turning often. Brush the saté with a little of the sauce and serve hot, with onion, cucumber wedges, if using, rice shapes and the sauce.

COOK'S TIP
Compressed rice shapes are easy to make. Cook two 115g/4oz packets of boil-in-the-bag rice in a large pan of salted, boiling water and simmer for 1¼ hours until the cooked rice fills each bag like a plump cushion. The bags must be covered with water throughout. When cool, cut each rice slab horizontally in half, then into diamond shapes using a sharp, wetted knife.

Energy 33kcal/139kJ; Protein 3.5g; Carbohydrate 0.6g, of which sugars 0.3g; Fat 1.9g, of which saturates 0.9g, of which polyunsaturates 0.1g; Cholesterol 13mg; Calcium 2mg; Fibre 0.1g; Sodium 86mg.

BAKED CINNAMON MEAT LOAF ★

THIS TYPE OF MEAT LOAF IS USUALLY SERVED AS A SUPPER OR LIGHT LUNCH, WITH A CRUSTY BAGUETTE. ACCOMPANIED WITH EITHER TART PICKLES OR A CRUNCHY SALAD, AND SPLASHED WITH PIQUANT SAUCE, IT IS LIGHT AND TASTY.

SERVES FOUR TO SIX

INGREDIENTS

30ml/2 tbsp *nuoc mam*
25ml/1½ tbsp ground cinnamon
10ml/2 tsp sugar
5ml/1 tsp ground black pepper
15ml/1 tbsp potato starch
450g/1lb lean minced (ground) pork
30ml/2 tbsp sunflower oil
2–3 shallots, very finely chopped
spray sunflower oil, for greasing
nuoc cham, for drizzling
red chilli strips, to garnish
bread or noodles, to serve

COOK'S TIPS
• Serve the meat loaf as a nibble with drinks by cutting it into bitesize squares or fingers.
• Serve with a piquant sauce for dipping.
• Cut the meat loaf into wedges and take on a picnic to eat with bread and pickles or chutney.
• Fry slices of meat loaf until browned and serve with fried eggs.

VARIATION
For a delicious meat loaf that is even lower in fat, replace the lean minced (ground) pork with chicken breast fillets.

1 In a large bowl, mix together the *nuoc mam*, ground cinnamon, sugar and ground black pepper. Sprinkle over the potato starch and beat until the mixture is smooth.

2 Add the minced pork, the oil, and the very finely chopped shallots to the bowl and mix thoroughly. Cover with clear film (plastic wrap) and put in the refrigerator for 3–4 hours.

3 Preheat the oven to 180°C/350°F/Gas 4. Lightly oil a baking tin (pan) and spread the pork and shallot mixture in the tin in an even layer – when pressed, the potato starch should mean it feels springy.

4 Cover with foil and bake in the oven for 35–40 minutes. If you want the top to turn brown and crunchy, remove the foil for the last 10 minutes.

5 Turn the meat loaf out on to a board and slice it into strips. Drizzle the strips with *nuoc cham*, and serve them hot with bread or noodles.

Energy 158kcal/661kJ; Protein 16.8g; Carbohydrate 7.7g, of which sugars 4.6g; Fat 6.8g, of which saturates 1.5g, of which polyunsaturates 2.9g; Cholesterol 47mg; Calcium 19mg; Fibre 0.8g; Sodium 54mg.

LARP OF CHIANG MAI ★

CHIANG MAI IS A CITY IN THE NORTH-EAST OF THAILAND. THE CITY IS CULTURALLY VERY CLOSE TO LAOS AND FAMOUS FOR ITS CHICKEN SALAD, WHICH WAS ORIGINALLY CALLED "LAAP" OR "LARP". DUCK, BEEF OR PORK CAN BE USED INSTEAD OF CHICKEN.

SERVES FOUR

INGREDIENTS

  450g/1lb minced (ground) chicken
    or pork
  1 lemon grass stalk, root trimmed
  3 kaffir lime leaves, finely chopped
  4 fresh red chillies, seeded
    and chopped
  60ml/4 tbsp lime juice
  30ml/2 tbsp Thai fish sauce
  15ml/1 tbsp roasted ground rice (see
    Cook's Tip)
  2 spring onions (scallions), chopped
  30ml/2 tbsp fresh coriander
    (cilantro) leaves
  thinly sliced kaffir lime leaves, mixed
    salad leaves and fresh mint sprigs,
    to garnish

1 Heat a large non-stick frying pan. Add the minced chicken or pork and moisten with a little water. Stir constantly over a medium heat for 7–10 minutes until it is cooked. Meanwhile, cut off the lower 5cm/2in of the lemon grass stalk and chop finely.

2 Transfer the cooked chicken to a bowl and add the chopped lemon grass, lime leaves, chillies, lime juice, fish sauce, ground rice, spring onions and coriander. Mix thoroughly.

3 Spoon the chicken mixture into a salad bowl. Sprinkle sliced kaffir lime leaves over the top and garnish with salad leaves and sprigs of mint.

COOK'S TIP
Use glutinous rice for the roasted ground rice. Put the rice in a frying pan and dry-fry it until golden brown. Remove and grind to a powder, using a pestle and mortar or a food processor. When the rice is cold, store it in a glass jar in a cool and dry place.

THAI BEEF SALAD ★★

A HEARTY AND HEALTHY MAIN MEAL SALAD, PACKED WITH GREEN VEGETABLES, THIS COMBINES TENDER STRIPS OF STEAK WITH A WONDERFUL CHILLI AND LIME DRESSING.

SERVES FOUR

INGREDIENTS

  2 sirloin steaks, each
    about 400g/14oz
  1 lemon grass stalk, root trimmed
  1 red onion or 4 Thai shallots,
    thinly sliced
  1/2 cucumber, cut into strips
  30ml/2 tbsp chopped spring
    onion (scallion)
  juice of 2 limes
  15–30ml/1–2 tbsp Thai
    fish sauce
  Chinese mustard cress, salad cress, or
    fresh coriander (cilantro) to garnish

COOK'S TIP
Look out for gui chai leaves in Thai and Asian groceries. These look like very thin spring onions (scallions) and are often used as a substitute for the more familiar vegetable.

1 Pan-fry or grill (broil) the steaks in a large, heavy frying pan over a medium heat, for 6–8 minutes for medium-rare and about 10 minutes for well done. Remove from the pan and allow to rest for 10–15 minutes. Meanwhile, cut off the lower 5cm/2in from the lemon grass stalk and chop it finely.

2 When the meat is cool, slice it thinly and put the slices in a large bowl.

3 Add the sliced onion or shallots, cucumber, lemon grass and chopped spring onion to the meat slices.

4 Toss the salad and season with the lime juice and fish sauce to taste. Transfer the salad to a serving bowl or plate and serve at room temperature or chilled, garnished with the Chinese mustard cress, salad cress or coriander leaves.

Top: Energy 163kcal/682kJ; Protein 25.3g; Carbohydrate 4.4g, of which sugars 1.2g; Fat 4.8g, of which saturates 1.6g, of which polyunsaturates 0.8g; Cholesterol 71mg; Calcium 53mg; Fibre 1.1g; Sodium 620mg.
Bottom: Energy 186kcal/774kJ; Protein 23.3g; Carbohydrate 2g, of which sugars 1.6g; Fat 9.4g, of which saturates 3.8g, of which polyunsaturates 0.4g; Cholesterol 58mg; Calcium 16mg; Fibre 0.4g; Sodium 333mg.

RICE AND NOODLES

Low in fat and high in carbohydrate, rice and noodles form the
bulk of most meals in Thailand and South-east Asia, combined
with a healthy proportion of vegetables and just small amounts
of protein in the shape of meat, fish or tofu. Universally low
in saturated fat, many of these recipes contain all the delicious
flavours of classic Thai cooking and less than 1 gram per serving,
including Garlic and Ginger Rice with Coriander, Stir-fried
Noodles in Seafood Sauce and traditional Mixed Meat Noodles.

COCONUT RICE ★

THIS RICH DISH IS OFTEN SERVED WITH A TANGY PAPAYA SALAD TO BALANCE THE SWEETNESS OF THE
COCONUT MILK AND SUGAR. IT IS ONE OF THOSE COMFORTING TREATS THAT EVERYONE ENJOYS.

SERVES SIX

INGREDIENTS
   250ml/8fl oz/1 cup water
   475ml/16fl oz/2 cups reduced-fat
   coconut milk
   2.5ml/½ tsp salt
   30ml/2 tbsp granulated sugar
   450g/1lb/2⅔ cups jasmine rice

COOK'S TIP
For a special occasion serve in a halved
papaya and garnish with thin shreds of
fresh coconut. Use a vegetable peeler to
pare the coconut finely.

1 Place the measured water, coconut
milk, salt and sugar in a heavy pan.
Wash the rice in several changes of
cold water until it runs clear.

2 Add the jasmine rice, cover tightly
with a lid and bring to the boil over a
medium heat. Reduce the heat to low
and simmer gently, without lifting the lid
unnecessarily, for 15–20 minutes, until
the rice is tender and cooked through.
Test it by biting a grain.

3 Turn off the heat and leave the rice to
rest in the pan, still covered with the lid,
for a further 5–10 minutes.

4 Gently fluff up the rice grains with
chopsticks or a fork before transferring
it to a warmed dish and serving.

Energy 306kcal/1286kJ; Protein 5.8g; Carbohydrate 69g, of which sugars 9.1g; Fat 0.6g, of which saturates 0.2g, of which polyunsaturates 0g; Cholesterol 0mg; Calcium 40mg; Fibre 0g; Sodium 218mg.

INDONESIAN COCONUT RICE ★

*THIS WAY OF COOKING RICE IS VERY POPULAR THROUGHOUT THE WHOLE OF SOUTH-EAST ASIA.
COCONUT RICE GOES PARTICULARLY WELL WITH FISH, CHICKEN AND PORK.*

SERVES SIX

INGREDIENTS

350g/12oz/1¾ cups Thai fragrant rice
400ml/14fl oz can reduced-fat
 coconut milk
300ml/½ pint/1¼ cups water
2.5ml/½ tsp ground coriander
5cm/2in cinnamon stick
1 lemon grass stalk, bruised
1 bay leaf
salt
crisp fried onions, to garnish

1 Put the rice in a strainer and rinse
thoroughly under cold water. Drain well,
then put in a pan. Pour in the coconut
milk and water. Add the coriander,
cinnamon stick, lemon grass and bay
leaf. Season with salt. Bring to the boil,
then lower the heat, cover and simmer
for 8–10 minutes.

2 Lift the lid and check that all the
liquid has been absorbed, then fork
the rice through carefully, removing
the cinnamon stick, lemon grass and
bay leaf.

3 Cover the pan with a tight-fitting
lid and continue to cook the rice
over the lowest possible heat for
3–5 minutes more. Take care that
the pan does not scorch.

4 Pile the rice on to a warm serving
dish and serve garnished with the
crisp fried onions.

VARIATION
For a quick and easy healthy supper,
stir in strips of freshly cooked skinless
chicken breast and peas 5-6 minutes
before serving and heat through.

COOK'S TIP
When bringing the rice to the boil, stir
it frequently to prevent it from settling
on the bottom of the pan. Once the rice
is nearly tender, continue to cook over
a very low heat or just leave to stand
for 5 minutes.

Energy 226kcal/945kJ; Protein 4.6g; Carbohydrate 49.9g, of which sugars 3.4g; Fat 0.6g, of which saturates 0.1g, of which polyunsaturates 0g; Cholesterol 0mg; Calcium 39mg; Fibre 0.2g; Sodium 75mg.

GARLIC AND GINGER RICE WITH CORIANDER ★

IN VIETNAM AND CAMBODIA, WHEN RICE IS SERVED ON THE SIDE, IT IS USUALLY STEAMED AND PLAIN, OR FRAGRANT WITH THE FLAVOURS OF GINGER AND HERBS. THE COMBINATION OF GARLIC AND GINGER IS POPULAR IN BOTH COUNTRIES AND COMPLEMENTS ALMOST ANY VEGETABLE, FISH OR MEAT DISH.

SERVES SIX

INGREDIENTS

 15ml/1 tbsp sunflower oil
 2–3 garlic cloves,
  finely chopped
 25g/1oz fresh root ginger,
  finely chopped
 225g/8oz/generous 1 cup
  long grain rice, rinsed in
  several bowls of cold water
  and drained
 900ml/1½ pints/3¾ cups
  chicken stock
 a bunch of fresh coriander (cilantro)
  leaves, finely chopped
 a bunch of fresh basil and mint,
  (optional), finely chopped

1 Heat the oil in a clay pot or heavy pan. Stir in the garlic and ginger and fry until golden. Stir in the rice and allow it to absorb the flavours for 1–2 minutes. Pour in the stock and stir to make sure the rice doesn't stick. Bring the stock to the boil, then reduce the heat.

2 Sprinkle the coriander over the surface of the stock, cover the pan, and leave to cook gently for 20–25 minutes, until the rice has absorbed all the liquid. Turn off the heat and gently fluff up the rice to mix in the coriander. Cover and leave to infuse for 10 minutes before serving.

Energy 162kcal/677kJ; Protein 3.7g; Carbohydrate 31.5g, of which sugars 0.3g; Fat 2.2g, of which saturates 0.2g, of which polyunsaturates 1.2g; Cholesterol 0mg; Calcium 25mg; Fibre 0.8g; Sodium 3mg.

SOUTHERN-SPICED CHILLI RICE ★

ALTHOUGH PLAIN STEAMED RICE IS SERVED AT ALMOST EVERY MEAL THROUGHOUT SOUTH-EAST ASIA, MANY FAMILIES LIKE TO SNEAK IN A LITTLE SPICE TOO. A BURST OF CHILLI FOR FIRE, TURMERIC FOR COLOUR, AND CORIANDER FOR ITS COOLING FLAVOUR, ARE ALL THAT'S NEEDED.

SERVES FOUR

INGREDIENTS
  15ml/1 tbsp sunflower oil
  2–3 green or red Thai chillies,
    seeded and finely chopped
  2 garlic cloves, finely chopped
  2.5cm/1in fresh root ginger, chopped
  5ml/1 tsp sugar
  10–15ml/2–3 tsp ground turmeric
  225g/8oz/generous 1 cup long
    grain rice
  30ml/2 tbsp *nuoc mam*
  600ml/1 pint/2½ cups water
  1 bunch of fresh coriander
    (cilantro), stalks removed, leaves
    finely chopped
  salt and ground black pepper

1 Heat the oil in a heavy pan. Stir in the chillies, garlic and ginger with the sugar. As they begin to colour, stir in the turmeric. Add the rice, coating it well, then pour in the *nuoc mam* and the water – the liquid should sit about 2.5cm/1in above the rice.

2 Tip the rice on to a serving dish. Add some of the coriander and lightly toss together using a fork. Garnish with the remaining coriander.

COOK'S TIP
This rice goes well with grilled and stir-fried fish and shellfish dishes, but you can serve it as an alternative to plain rice. Add extra chillies, if you like.

3 Season with salt and ground black pepper and bring the liquid to the boil. Reduce the heat, cover and simmer for about 25 minutes, or until the water has been absorbed. Remove from the heat and leave the rice to steam for a further 10 minutes.

Energy 247kcal/1032kJ; Protein 5.5g; Carbohydrate 48.3g, of which sugars 1.5g; Fat 3.3g, of which saturates 0.4g, of which polyunsaturates 1.8g; Cholesterol 0mg; Calcium 39mg; Fibre 1.1g; Sodium 5mg.

FESTIVE RICE ★

THIS PRETTY THAI DISH IS TRADITIONALLY SHAPED INTO A CONE AND SURROUNDED BY A VARIETY OF
ACCOMPANIMENTS BEFORE BEING SERVED. SERVE AT A HEALTHY SUMMERTIME LUNCH.

2 Heat the oil in a frying pan with a lid. Cook the garlic, onions and turmeric over a low heat for 2–3 minutes, until the onions have softened. Add the rice and stir well to coat in oil.

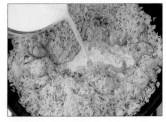

3 Pour in the water and coconut milk and add the lemon grass. Bring to the boil, stirring. Cover the pan and cook gently for 12 minutes, or until all the liquid has been absorbed by the rice.

SERVES EIGHT

INGREDIENTS

    450g/1lb/2⅔ cups jasmine rice
    30ml/2 tbsp sunflower oil
    2 garlic cloves, crushed
    2 onions, thinly sliced
    2.5ml/½ tsp ground turmeric
    750ml/1¼ pints/3 cups water
    400ml/14fl oz can reduced-fat
      coconut milk
    1–2 lemon grass stalks, bruised
For the accompaniments
    omelette strips
    2 fresh red chillies, shredded
    cucumber chunks
    tomato wedges
    fried onions
    prawn (shrimp) crackers

1 Put the jasmine rice in a large strainer and rinse it thoroughly under cold water. Drain well.

COOK'S TIP

Jasmine rice is widely available in most supermarkets and Asian stores. It is also known as Thai fragrant rice.

4 Remove the pan from the heat and lift the lid. Cover with a clean dish towel, replace the lid and leave to stand in a warm place for 15 minutes. Remove the lemon grass, mound the rice mixture in a cone on a serving platter and garnish with the accompaniments, then serve.

Energy 224kcal/939kJ; Protein 4.8g; Carbohydrate 49.5g, of which sugars 4g; Fat 0.6g, of which saturates 0.1g, of which polyunsaturates 0g; Cholesterol 0mg; Calcium 44mg; Fibre 0.7g; Sodium 58mg.

BROWN RICE <u>WITH</u> LIME <u>AND</u> LEMON GRASS ★

IT IS UNUSUAL TO FIND BROWN RICE GIVEN THE THAI TREATMENT, BUT THE NUTTY FLAVOUR OF THE GRAINS IS ENHANCED BY THE FRAGRANCE OF LIMES AND LEMON GRASS IN THIS DELICIOUS DISH.

SERVES FOUR

INGREDIENTS

2 limes
1 lemon grass stalk
225g/8oz/generous 1 cup brown long grain rice
15ml/1 tbsp olive oil
1 onion, chopped
2.5cm/1in piece fresh root ginger, peeled and finely chopped
7.5ml/1½ tsp coriander seeds
7.5ml/1½ tsp cumin seeds
750ml/1¼ pints/3 cups vegetable stock
60ml/4 tbsp chopped fresh coriander (cilantro)
spring onion (scallion) green and toasted coconut strips, to garnish
lime wedges, to serve

3 Heat the oil in a large pan. Add the onion, ginger, coriander and cumin seeds, lemon grass and lime rind and cook over a low heat for 2–3 minutes.

4 Add the rice to the pan and cook, stirring constantly, for 1 minute, then pour in the stock and bring to the boil. Reduce the heat to very low and cover the pan. Cook gently for 30 minutes, then check the rice. If it is still crunchy, cover the pan and cook for 3–5 minutes more. Remove from the heat.

5 Stir in the fresh coriander, fluff up the rice grains with a fork, cover the pan and leave to stand for 10 minutes. Transfer to a warmed dish, garnish with spring onion green and toasted coconut strips, and serve with lime wedges.

1 Pare the limes, using a cannelle knife (zester) or fine grater, taking care to avoid cutting the bitter pith. Set the rind aside. Finely chop the lower portion of the lemon grass stalk and set it aside.

2 Rinse the rice in plenty of cold water until the water runs clear. Tip it into a sieve and drain thoroughly.

Energy 235kcal/996kJ; Protein 4.3g; Carbohydrate 47.3g, of which sugars 1.9g; Fat 4.5g, of which saturates 0.8g, of which polyunsaturates 0.8g; Cholesterol 0mg; Calcium 35mg; Fibre 1.9g; Sodium 6mg.

JASMINE RICE WITH PRAWNS AND THAI BASIL ★

THAI BASIL (BAI GRAPAO), ALSO KNOWN AS HOLY BASIL, HAS A UNIQUE, PUNGENT FLAVOUR THAT IS BOTH SPICY AND SHARP. IT CAN BE FOUND IN MOST ASIAN FOOD MARKETS.

SERVES SIX

INGREDIENTS
  15ml/1 tbsp sunflower oil
  1 egg, beaten
  1 onion, chopped
  15ml/1 tbsp chopped garlic
  15ml/1 tbsp shrimp paste
  1kg/2¼lb/4 cups cooked jasmine rice
  350g/12oz cooked shelled prawns
    (shrimp)
  50g/2oz thawed frozen peas
  oyster sauce, to taste
  2 spring onions (scallions), chopped
  15–20 Thai basil leaves, roughly
    snipped, plus an extra sprig,
    to garnish

1 Heat 15ml/1 tbsp of the oil in a wok or frying pan. Add the beaten egg and swirl it around to set like a thin omelette.

2 Cook the omelette (on one side only) over a gentle heat until golden. Slide the omelette on to a board, roll up and cut into thin strips. Set aside.

3 Heat the remaining oil in the wok or pan, add the onion and garlic and stir-fry for 2–3 minutes. Stir in the shrimp paste and mix well until thoroughly combined.

4 Add the rice, prawns and peas and toss and stir together, until everything is heated through.

5 Season with oyster sauce to taste, taking great care as the shrimp paste is salty. Mix in the spring onions and basil leaves. Transfer to a serving dish and top with the strips of omelette. Serve, garnished with a sprig of basil.

Energy 311kcal/1316kJ; Protein 16.3g; Carbohydrate 52.6g, of which sugars 0.3g; Fat 5.4g, of which saturates 1.1g, of which polyunsaturates 2.2g; Cholesterol 145mg; Calcium 84mg; Fibre 0.6g; Sodium 125mg.

THAI FRIED RICE ★★

THIS SUBSTANTIAL AND TASTY DISH IS BASED ON JASMINE RICE. DICED CHICKEN, RED PEPPER AND CORN KERNELS ADD COLOUR AND EXTRA FLAVOUR.

SERVES FOUR

INGREDIENTS
475ml/16fl oz/2 cups water
50g/2oz/½ cup coconut
  milk powder
350g/12oz/1¾ cups jasmine
  rice, rinsed
15ml/1 tbsp sunflower oil
2 garlic cloves, chopped
1 small onion, finely chopped
2.5cm/1in piece of fresh root ginger,
  peeled and grated
225g/8oz skinless, chicken breast
  fillets, cut into 1cm/½in dice
1 red (bell) pepper, seeded
  and sliced
115g/4oz/1 cup drained canned
  whole kernel corn
5ml/1 tsp chilli oil
5ml/1 tsp hot curry powder
2 eggs, beaten
salt
spring onion (scallion) shreds,
  to garnish

3 Push the onion mixture to the sides of the wok, add the chicken to the centre and stir-fry for 2 minutes. Add the rice and toss well. Stir-fry over a high heat for about 3 minutes more, until the chicken is cooked through.

4 Stir in the sliced red pepper, corn, chilli oil and curry powder, with salt to taste. Toss over the heat for 1 minute. Stir in the beaten eggs and cook for 1 minute more. Garnish with the spring onion shreds and serve.

1 Pour the water into a pan and whisk in the coconut milk powder. Add the rice and bring to the boil. Reduce the heat, cover and cook for 12 minutes, or until the rice is tender and the liquid has been absorbed. Spread the rice on a baking sheet and leave until cold.

2 Heat the oil in a wok, add the garlic, onion and ginger and stir-fry over a medium heat for 2 minutes.

COOK'S TIP
It is important that the rice is completely cold before being fried.

Energy 508kcal/2127kJ; Protein 24.7g; Carbohydrate 83.9g, of which sugars 8.7g; Fat 8g, of which saturates 1.6g, of which polyunsaturates 2.7g; Cholesterol 135mg; Calcium 57mg; Fibre 1.3g; Sodium 204mg.

PLAIN NOODLES WITH FOUR FLAVOURS ★

A WONDERFULLY SIMPLE WAY OF SERVING NOODLES, THIS DISH ALLOWS EACH INDIVIDUAL DINER TO
SEASON THEIR OWN, SPRINKLING OVER THE FOUR FLAVOURS AS THEY LIKE. FLAVOURINGS ARE ALWAYS
PUT OUT IN LITTLE BOWLS WHENEVER NOODLES ARE SERVED.

SERVES FOUR

INGREDIENTS
    4 small fresh red or green chillies
    60ml/4 tbsp Thai fish sauce
    60ml/4 tbsp rice vinegar
    granulated sugar
    mild or hot chilli powder
    350g/12oz rice noodles

1 Prepare the four flavours. For the first, finely chop 2 small red or green chillies, discarding the seeds or leaving them in, depending on how hot you like your flavouring. Place them in a small bowl and add the Thai fish sauce.

2 For the second flavour, chop the remaining chillies finely and mix them with the rice vinegar in a small bowl. Put the sugar and chilli powder in separate small bowls.

3 Cook the noodles until tender, following the instructions on the packet. Drain well, tip into a large bowl and serve immediately with the four flavours handed separately.

Energy 321kcal/1341kJ; Protein 4.5g; Carbohydrate 72.4g, of which sugars 1g; Fat 0.2g, of which saturates 0g, of which polyunsaturates 0g; Cholesterol 0mg; Calcium 12mg; Fibre 0.2g; Sodium 278mg.

THAI NOODLES ᵂᴵᵀᴴ CHINESE CHIVES ★★

THIS RECIPE REQUIRES A LITTLE TIME FOR PREPARATION, BUT THE COOKING TIME IS VERY FAST.
EVERYTHING IS COOKED IN A HOT WOK AND SHOULD BE EATEN IMMEDIATELY. THIS IS A FILLING
AND TASTY VEGETARIAN DISH, IDEAL FOR A WEEKEND LUNCH.

SERVES FOUR

INGREDIENTS
  350g/12oz dried rice noodles
  1cm/½in piece fresh root ginger,
    peeled and grated
  30ml/2 tbsp light soy sauce
  225g/8oz Quorn (mycoprotein),
    cut into small cubes
  15ml/1 tbsp sunflower oil
  2 garlic cloves, crushed
  1 large onion, cut into
    thin wedges
  115g/4oz fried tofu, thinly sliced
  1 fresh green chilli, seeded and
    thinly sliced
  175g/6oz/2 cups beansprouts
  2 large bunches garlic chives, total
    weight about 115g/4oz, cut into
    5cm/2in lengths
  30ml/2 tbsp roasted peanuts, ground
  30ml/2 tbsp dark soy sauce
  30ml/2 tbsp chopped fresh coriander
    (cilantro), and 1 lemon, cut into
    wedges, to garnish

1 Place the noodles in a bowl, cover with warm water and leave to soak for 30 minutes. Drain and set aside.

2 Mix the ginger and light soy sauce in a bowl. Add the Quorn, then set aside for 10 minutes. Drain, reserving the marinade.

3 Heat half the oil in a frying pan and cook the garlic for a few seconds. Add the Quorn and stir-fry for 3–4 minutes. Using a slotted spoon, transfer to a plate and set aside.

4 Heat the remaining oil in the pan and stir-fry the onion for 3–4 minutes, until softened and tinged with brown. Add the tofu and chilli, stir-fry briefly and then add the noodles. Stir-fry over a medium heat for 4–5 minutes.

5 Stir in the beansprouts, garlic chives and most of the ground peanuts, reserving a little for the garnish. Stir well, then add the Quorn, the dark soy sauce and the reserved marinade.

6 When hot, spoon on to serving plates and garnish with the remaining ground peanuts, the coriander and lemon.

Energy 444kcal/1857kJ; Protein 16g; Carbohydrate 77.6g, of which sugars 4.3g; Fat 6.5g, of which saturates 0.9g, of which polyunsaturates 3.2g; Cholesterol 0mg; Calcium 230mg; Fibre 5g; Sodium 1227mg.

CURRIED RICE VERMICELLI ★

SIMPLE AND SPEEDILY PREPARED, THIS LIGHTLY FLAVOURED RICE NOODLE DISH WITH VEGETABLES AND PRAWNS IS ALMOST A COMPLETE MEAL IN A BOWL.

SERVES FOUR

INGREDIENTS
    225g/8oz/2 cups dried rice vermicelli
    10ml/2 tsp sunflower oil
    1 egg, lightly beaten
    2 garlic cloves, finely chopped
    1 large fresh red or green chilli,
      seeded and finely chopped
    15ml/1 tbsp medium curry powder
    1 red (bell) pepper, thinly sliced
    1 green (bell) pepper, thinly sliced
    1 carrot, cut into matchsticks
    1.5ml/¼ tsp salt
    60ml/4 tbsp vegetable stock
    115g/4oz cooked peeled prawns
      (shrimp), thawed if frozen
    75g/3oz lean ham, cut into cubes
    15ml/1 tbsp light soy sauce

1 Soak the rice vermicelli in a bowl of boiling water for 4 minutes, or according to the instructions on the packet, then drain thoroughly through a sieve or colander and set aside. Cover the bowl with a damp cloth or with clear film (plastic wrap) so that the vermicelli does not dry out.

2 Heat 5ml/1 tsp of the oil in a non-stick frying pan or wok. Add the egg and scramble until set, stirring with a pair of wooden chopsticks. Remove the egg with a slotted spoon and set aside.

3 Heat the remaining oil in the clean pan. Stir-fry the garlic and chilli for a few seconds, then stir in the curry powder. Cook for 1 minute, stirring, then stir in the peppers, carrot sticks, salt and stock.

4 Bring the mixture to the boil. Add the prawns, ham, scrambled egg, rice vermicelli and soy sauce. Mix well. Cook, stirring, until all the liquid has been absorbed and the mixture is hot. Serve immediately.

Energy 306kcal/1281kJ; Protein 16g; Carbohydrate 50.9g, of which sugars 6.5g; Fat 4.3g, of which saturates 0.9g, of which polyunsaturates 1.4g; Cholesterol 115mg; Calcium 56mg; Fibre 1.8g; Sodium 309mg.

STIR-FRIED NOODLES IN SEAFOOD SAUCE ★

THE ADDITION OF EXTRA SPECIAL INGREDIENTS SUCH AS CRAB AND ASPARAGUS IN THIS DISH CAN MAKE A SIMPLE STIR-FRY A REAL TREAT THAT IS STILL VIRTUALLY FAT FREE.

SERVES EIGHT

INGREDIENTS

225g/8oz fresh or dried Chinese egg noodles
8 spring onions (scallions), cleaned and trimmed
8 asparagus spears, plus extra steamed asparagus spears, to serve (optional)
15ml/1 tbsp sunflower oil
5cm/2in piece fresh root ginger, peeled and cut into very fine matchsticks
3 garlic cloves, chopped
60ml/4 tbsp oyster sauce
450g/1lb cooked crab meat (all white, or two-thirds white and one-third brown)
30ml/2 tbsp rice wine vinegar
15–30ml/1–2 tbsp light soy sauce

1 Put the noodles in a large pan or wok, cover with lightly salted boiling water, place a lid on top and simmer for 3–4 minutes, or for the time suggested on the packet. Drain and set aside.

2 Cut off the green spring onion tops and slice them thinly. Set aside. Cut the white parts into 2cm/¾in lengths and quarter them lengthways. Cut the asparagus spears on the diagonal into 2cm/¾in pieces.

3 Heat the oil in a pan or wok until very hot, then add the ginger, garlic and white spring onion batons. Stir-fry over a high heat for 1 minute. Add the oyster sauce, crab meat, rice wine vinegar and soy sauce to taste. Stir-fry for about 2 minutes, until the crab and sauce are hot. Add the noodles and toss until heated through. At the last moment, toss in the spring onion tops and serve with a few extra asparagus spears, if you like.

Energy 179kcal/756kJ; Protein 14.1g; Carbohydrate 22.9g, of which sugars 3.1g; Fat 4.1g, of which saturates 0.9g, of which polyunsaturates 1.2g; Cholesterol 49mg; Calcium 82mg; Fibre 1.1g; Sodium 617mg.

MIXED MEAT NOODLES ★

A CLASSIC SOUTH-EAST ASIAN DISH THAT ORIGINATED IN SINGAPORE AND HAS BEEN ADOPTED AND ADAPTED BY ITS NEIGHBOURING COUNTRIES. THE NOODLES ARE STANDARD STREET AND CAFÉ FOOD, AN IDEAL SNACK FOR ANYONE FEELING A LITTLE PECKISH.

SERVES FOUR

INGREDIENTS

15ml/1 tbsp sesame oil
1 onion, finely chopped
3 garlic cloves, finely chopped
3–4 green or red Thai chillies,
  seeded and finely chopped
4cm/1½in fresh root ginger,
  peeled and finely chopped
6 spring onions (scallions), chopped
1 skinless chicken breast fillet,
  cut into bitesize strips
90g/3½oz lean pork, cut into
  bitesize strips
90g/3½oz prawns (shrimp), shelled
2 tomatoes, skinned, seeded
  and chopped
30ml/2 tbsp tamarind paste
15ml/1 tbsp *nuoc mam*
grated rind and juice of 1 lime
10ml/2 tsp sugar
150ml/¼ pint/⅔ cup water or fish stock
225g/8oz fresh rice sticks (vermicelli)
salt and ground black pepper
1 bunch each fresh basil and mint,
  and *nuoc cham*, to serve

1 Heat a wok or heavy pan and add the sesame oil. Stir in the finely chopped onion, garlic, chillies and ginger, and cook until they begin to colour. Add the spring onions and cook for 1 minute, add the chicken and pork, and cook for 1–2 minutes, then stir in the prawns.

2 Add the tomatoes, followed by the tamarind paste, *nuoc mam*, lime rind and juice, and sugar to the pan and stir well. Pour in the water or fish stock, and stir again before cooking gently for 2–3 minutes. Bubble up the liquid to reduce it.

VARIATIONS
• At noodle stalls in street markets in Thailand and South-east Asia, batches of cold, cooked noodles are kept ready to add to whatever delicious concoction is cooking in the wok.
• At home, you can make this dish with any kind of noodles – egg or rice, fresh or dried.
• Cured Chinese sausage and snails, or strips of squid, are sometimes added to the mixture to ring the changes.

3 Meanwhile, toss the noodles in a large pan of boiling water and cook for a few minutes until tender.

4 Drain the noodles and add to the chicken and prawn mixture. Season with salt and ground black pepper.

5 Serve immediately, with basil and mint leaves sprinkled over the top, and drizzled with spoonfuls of *nuoc cham*.

COOK'S TIP
It's important to serve this dish immediately once the noodles have been added, otherwise they will go soft.

Energy 314kcal/1316kJ; Protein 19.2g; Carbohydrate 50.3g, of which sugars 5.9g; Fat 4g, of which saturates 0.6g, of which polyunsaturates 1.5g; Cholesterol 70mg; Calcium 74mg; Fibre 1.6g; Sodium 81mg.

STEAMED VEGETABLES WITH CHIANG MAI SPICY DIP ★

IN THAILAND, STEAMED VEGETABLES ARE OFTEN PARTNERED WITH RAW ONES TO CREATE THE CONTRASTING TEXTURES THAT ARE SUCH A FEATURE OF THE NATIONAL CUISINE. BY HAPPY COINCIDENCE, IT IS AN EXTREMELY HEALTHY WAY TO SERVE THEM.

SERVES FOUR

INGREDIENTS
    1 head broccoli, divided
    into florets
    130g/4½oz 1 cup green
    beans, trimmed
    130g/4½oz asparagus, trimmed
    ½ head cauliflower, divided
    into florets
    8 baby corn cobs
    130g/4½oz mangetouts (snow peas)
    or sugar snap peas
    salt
For the dip
    1 fresh green chilli, seeded
    4 garlic cloves, peeled
    4 shallots, peeled
    2 tomatoes, halved
    5 pea aubergines (eggplants)
    30ml/2 tbsp lemon juice
    30ml/2 tbsp soy sauce
    2.5ml/½ tsp salt
    5ml/1 tsp granulated sugar

COOK'S TIP
Cauliflower varieties with pale green florets have a more delicate flavour than those with white florets.

1 Place the broccoli, green beans, asparagus and cauliflower in a steamer and steam over boiling water for about 4 minutes, until just tender but still with a "bite". Transfer them to a bowl and add the corn cobs and mangetouts or sugar snap peas. Season to taste with a little salt. Toss to mix, then set aside.

2 Make the dip. Preheat the grill (broiler). Wrap the chilli, garlic cloves, shallots, tomatoes and aubergines in a foil package. Grill (broil) for 10 minutes, until the vegetables have softened, turning the package over once or twice.

3 Unwrap the foil and tip its contents into a mortar or food processor. Add the lemon juice, soy sauce, salt and sugar. Pound with a pestle or process to a fairly liquid paste.

4 Scrape the dip into a serving bowl or four individual bowls. Serve, surrounded by the steamed and raw vegetables.

VARIATIONS
You can use a combination of other vegetables if you like. Use pak choi (bok choy) instead of the cauliflower or substitute raw baby carrots for the corn cobs and mushrooms in place of the mangetouts (snow peas).

Energy 101kcal/422kJ; Protein 9.5g; Carbohydrate 11.9g, of which sugars 10.2g; Fat 2g, of which saturates 0.4g, of which polyunsaturates 1g; Cholesterol 0mg; Calcium 98mg; Fibre 6.7g; Sodium 1082mg.

MORNING GLORY <u>WITH</u> GARLIC <u>AND</u> SHALLOTS ★

MORNING GLORY GOES BY VARIOUS NAMES, INCLUDING WATER SPINACH, WATER CONVOLVULUS AND SWAMP CABBAGE. IT IS A GREEN LEAFY VEGETABLE WITH LONG JOINTED STEMS AND ARROW-SHAPED LEAVES. THE STEMS REMAIN CRUNCHY WHILE THE LEAVES WILT LIKE SPINACH WHEN COOKED.

SERVES FOUR

INGREDIENTS
    2 bunches morning glory, total weight
    about 250g/9oz, trimmed and
    coarsely chopped into 2.5cm/
    1in lengths
    15ml/1 tbsp sunflower oil
    4 shallots, thinly sliced
    6 large garlic cloves, thinly sliced
    sea salt
    1.5ml/¼ tsp dried chilli flakes

VARIATIONS
Use spinach instead of morning glory, or
substitute young spring greens (collards),
sprouting broccoli or Swiss chard.

1 Place the morning glory in a steamer
and steam over a pan of boiling water
for 30 seconds, until just wilted. If
necessary, cook it in batches. Place the
leaves in a bowl or spread them out on
a large serving plate.

2 Heat the oil in a wok and stir-fry the
shallots and garlic over a medium to
high heat until golden. Spoon the
mixture over the morning glory, sprinkle
with a little sea salt and the chilli flakes
and serve immediately.

Energy 58kcal/240kJ; Protein 2.9g; Carbohydrate 4.2g, of which sugars 2g; Fat 3.4g, of which saturates 0.4g, of which polyunsaturates 2.1g; Cholesterol 0mg; Calcium 113mg; Fibre 2g; Sodium 89mg.

STIR-FRIED PINEAPPLE <u>WITH</u> GINGER ★

THIS DISH MAKES AN INTERESTING ACCOMPANIMENT TO GRILLED MEAT OR STRONGLY FLAVOURED FISH SUCH AS TUNA OR SWORDFISH. IF THE IDEA SEEMS STRANGE, THINK OF IT AS RESEMBLING A FRESH MANGO CHUTNEY, BUT WITH PINEAPPLE AS THE PRINCIPAL INGREDIENT.

SERVES FOUR

INGREDIENTS
1 pineapple
15ml/1 tbsp sunflower oil
2 garlic cloves, finely chopped
2 shallots, finely chopped
5cm/2in piece fresh root ginger,
  peeled and finely shredded
30ml/2 tbsp light soy sauce
juice of ½ lime
1 large fresh red chilli, seeded and
  finely shredded

VARIATION
This also tastes excellent if peaches or nectarines are substituted for the diced pineapple. Use three or four, depending on their size.

1 Trim and peel the pineapple. Cut out the core and dice the flesh.

2 Heat the oil in a wok or frying pan. Stir-fry the garlic and shallots over a medium heat for 2–3 minutes, until golden. Do not let the garlic burn or the dish will taste bitter.

3 Add the pineapple. Stir-fry for about 2 minutes, or until the pineapple cubes start to turn golden on the edges.

4 Add the ginger, soy sauce, lime juice and chopped chilli. Toss together until well mixed. Cook over a low heat for a further 2 minutes, then serve.

Energy 119kcal/507kJ; Protein 1.3g; Carbohydrate 22.8g, of which sugars 22.4g; Fat 3.2g, of which saturates 0.4g, of which polyunsaturates 2g; Cholesterol 0mg; Calcium 42mg; Fibre 2.8g; Sodium 539mg.

PINEAPPLE WITH GINGER AND CHILLI ★

THROUGHOUT SOUTH-EAST ASIA, FRUIT IS OFTEN TREATED LIKE A VEGETABLE AND TOSSED IN A SALAD, OR STIR-FRIED, TO ACCOMPANY SPICY DISHES. IN THIS CAMBODIAN DISH, THE PINEAPPLE IS COMBINED WITH THE TANGY FLAVOURS OF GINGER AND CHILLI AND SERVED AS A SIDE DISH.

SERVES FOUR

INGREDIENTS

15ml/1 tbsp sunflower oil
2 garlic cloves, finely shredded
40g/1½oz fresh root ginger, peeled and finely shredded
2 red Thai chillies, seeded and finely shredded
1 pineapple, trimmed, peeled, cored and cut into bitesize chunks
15ml/1 tbsp *tuk trey*
30ml/2 tbsp soy sauce
15ml–30ml/1–2 tbsp sugar
15ml/1 tbsp roasted unsalted peanuts, finely chopped
1 lime, cut into quarters, to serve

1 Heat a large wok or heavy pan and add the sunflower oil. Stir in the finely shredded garlic, ginger and chilli. Stir-fry until they begin to colour, then add the pineapple chunks and stir-fry for a further 1–2 minutes, until the edges turn golden.

2 Add the *tuk trey*, soy sauce and sugar to taste and continue to stir-fry until the pineapple begins to caramelize.

3 Transfer to a serving dish, sprinkle with the roasted peanuts and serve with lime wedges.

Energy 136kcal/577kJ; Protein 2.1g; Carbohydrate 22.8g, of which sugars 22.5g; Fat 4.8g, of which saturates 0.6g, of which polyunsaturates 2.4g; Cholesterol 0mg; Calcium 41mg; Fibre 3g; Sodium 539mg.

SOUTHERN-STYLE YAM ★

THE FOOD OF SOUTHERN THAILAND IS NOTORIOUSLY HOT AND BECAUSE OF THE PROXIMITY TO THE BORDERS WITH MALAYSIA, THAILAND'S MUSLIM MINORITY ARE MOSTLY TO BE FOUND IN THIS AREA. THEY HAVE INTRODUCED RICHER CURRY FLAVOURS REMINISCENT OF INDIAN FOOD.

SERVES FOUR

INGREDIENTS
  90g/3½oz Chinese leaves (Chinese
    cabbage), shredded
  90g/3½oz/generous 1 cup
    beansprouts
  90g/3½oz/scant 1 cup green
    beans, trimmed
  90g/3½oz broccoli, preferably the
    purple sprouting variety, divided
    into florets
  15ml/1 tbsp sesame seeds, toasted
For the yam
  120ml/4fl oz/½ cup reduced-fat
    coconut milk
  5ml/1 tsp Thai red curry paste
  90g/3½oz/1¼ cups oyster
    mushrooms or field
    (portabello) mushrooms, sliced
  5ml/1 tsp ground turmeric
  5ml/1 tsp thick tamarind juice, made
    by mixing tamarind paste with
    warm water
  juice of ½ lemon
  60ml/4 tbsp light soy sauce
  5ml/1 tsp palm sugar or light
    muscovado (brown) sugar

1 Steam the shredded Chinese leaves, beansprouts, green beans and broccoli separately or blanch them in boiling water for 1 minute per batch. Drain, place in a serving bowl and leave to cool.

2 Make the yam. Pour half the coconut milk into a wok and heat gently for 2–3 minutes, until it separates. Stir in the red curry paste. Cook over a low heat for 30 seconds, until the mixture is fragrant.

3 Increase the heat to high and add the mushrooms to the wok or pan. Cook for a further 2–3 minutes.

4 Pour in the remaining coconut milk and add the ground turmeric, tamarind juice, lemon juice, soy sauce and sugar to the wok or pan. Mix thoroughly.

5 Pour the mixture over the prepared vegetables and toss well to combine. Sprinkle with the toasted sesame seeds and serve immediately.

COOK'S TIP
Oyster mushrooms need gentle handling. Tear large specimens apart and don't overcook them or they will be rubbery.

Energy 68kcal/286kJ; Protein 4g; Carbohydrate 7g, of which sugars 6.1g; Fat 2.9g, of which saturates 0.5g, of which polyunsaturates 1.3g; Cholesterol 0mg; Calcium 75mg; Fibre 2.4g; Sodium 1108mg.

FRAGRANT MUSHROOMS IN LETTUCE LEAVES ★

THIS QUICK AND EASY VEGETABLE DISH IS SERVED ON LETTUCE LEAF "SAUCERS" SO CAN BE EATEN WITH THE FINGERS — A GREAT TREAT FOR CHILDREN.

SERVES FOUR

INGREDIENTS

15ml/1 tbsp sunflower oil
2 garlic cloves, finely chopped
2 baby cos or romaine lettuces,
  or 2 Little Gem (Bibb) lettuces
1 lemon grass stalk, finely chopped
2 kaffir lime leaves, rolled in
  cylinders and thinly sliced
200g/7oz/3 cups oyster or chestnut
  mushrooms, sliced
1 small fresh red chilli, seeded
  and finely chopped
juice of ½ lemon
30ml/2 tbsp light soy sauce
5ml/1 tsp palm sugar or light
  muscovado (brown) sugar
small bunch fresh mint, leaves
  removed from the stalks

1 Heat a wok or large, heavy frying pan and add the sunflower oil. Add the finely chopped garlic and cook over a medium heat, stirring occasionally, until golden. Do not let it burn or it will taste bitter.

2 Meanwhile, separate the individual lettuce leaves and set aside.

3 Increase the heat under the wok or pan and add the lemon grass, lime leaves and sliced mushrooms. Stir-fry for about 2 minutes.

4 Add the chilli, lemon juice, soy sauce and sugar to the wok or pan. Toss the mixture over the heat to combine the ingredients together, then stir-fry for a further 2 minutes.

5 Arrange the lettuce leaves on a large plate. Spoon a small amount of the mushroom mixture on to each leaf, top with a mint leaf and serve.

Energy 52kcal/217kJ; Protein 2g; Carbohydrate 3.5g, of which sugars 3.3g; Fat 3.5g, of which saturates 0.5g, of which polyunsaturates 2.1g; Cholesterol 0mg; Calcium 45mg; Fibre 1.8g; Sodium 543mg.

FRIED VEGETABLES WITH NAM PRIK ★★

THIS DISH PROVIDES AN EASY WAY TO ACHIEVING FIVE FRUIT AND VEGETABLE PORTIONS A DAY AND IS SERVED WITH A PIQUANT DIP FOR MAXIMUM FLAVOUR.

SERVES SIX

INGREDIENTS

3 large (US extra large) eggs
1 aubergine (eggplant), halved
lengthways and cut into long,
thin slices
½ small butternut squash,
peeled, seeded and cut into
long, thin slices
2 courgettes (zucchini),
trimmed and cut into long,
thin slices
75ml/5 tbsp sunflower oil
salt and ground black pepper
nam prik or sweet chilli
sauce, to serve (see
Cook's Tip)

1 Beat the eggs in a large bowl. Add the aubergine, butternut squash and courgette slices. Toss the vegetables until coated all over in the egg, then season with salt and pepper.

2 Heat the oil in a wok. When it is hot, add the vegetables, one strip at a time, making sure that each strip has plenty of egg clinging to it. Do not cook more than eight strips at a time or the oil will cool down too much.

COOK'S TIP

Nam prik is quite a complex sauce, numbering dried shrimp, tiny aubergines (eggplant), shrimp paste and lime or lemon juice among its ingredients.

3 As each strip turns golden and is cooked, lift it out, using a wire basket or slotted spoon, and drain on kitchen paper. Keep hot while cooking the remaining vegetables. Transfer to a warmed dish and serve with the *nam prik* or sweet chilli sauce as a dip.

Energy 113kcal/468kJ; Protein 5.2g; Carbohydrate 3.6g, of which sugars 3.1g; Fat 8.8g, of which saturates 1.6g, of which polyunsaturates 4g; Cholesterol 95mg; Calcium 56mg; Fibre 2g; Sodium 36mg.

PICKLED VEGETABLE SALAD ★

EVERYDAY VIETNAMESE AND CAMBODIAN PICKLES GENERALLY CONSIST OF CUCUMBER, MOOLI AND CARROT — GREEN, WHITE AND ORANGE IN COLOUR — AND ARE SERVED FOR NIBBLING ON, AS PART OF THE TABLE SALAD, OR AS AN ACCOMPANIMENT TO GRILLED MEATS AND SHELLFISH.

SERVES SIX

INGREDIENTS
  300ml/½ pint/1¼ cups white
    rice vinegar
  90g/3½oz/½ cup sugar
  450g/1lb carrots, cut into 5cm/2in
    matchsticks
  450g/1lb mooli (daikon), halved,
    and cut into thin crescents
  600g/1lb 6oz cucumber, partially
    peeled in strips and cut into
    5cm/2in matchsticks
  15ml/1 tbsp salt

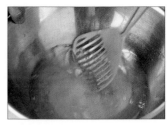

1 In a large bowl, whisk the vinegar with the sugar, until it dissolves.

2 Add the carrots and mooli to the vinegar mixture and toss well to coat. Cover them and place in the refrigerator for 24 hours, turning them occasionally.

3 Put the cucumber on a plate and sprinkle with the salt. Leave for 30 minutes, then rinse under cold water and drain well. Add to the carrot and mooli and toss well in the pickling liquid. Cover and refrigerate as before.

4 Lift the vegetables out of the pickling liquid to serve, or spoon them into a jar and store in the refrigerator.

Energy 104kcal/438kJ; Protein 1.8g; Carbohydrate 24.5g, of which sugars 24.1g; Fat 0.5g, of which saturates 0.2g, of which polyunsaturates 0.2g; Cholesterol 0mg; Calcium 59mg; Fibre 3.1g; Sodium 31mg.

HOT THAI PICKLED SHALLOTS ★

*PICKLING THAI SHALLOTS IN THIS WAY DEMANDS SOME PATIENCE, WHILE THE VINEGAR AND SPICES
WORK THEIR MAGIC, BUT THE RESULTS ARE DEFINITELY WORTH THE WAIT. THINLY SLICED, THE
SHALLOTS ARE OFTEN USED AS A CONDIMENT WITH SOUTH-EAST ASIAN MEALS.*

MAKES TWO TO THREE JARS

INGREDIENTS
  5–6 small red or green bird's
    eye chillies
  500g/1¼lb Thai pink
    shallots, peeled
  2 large garlic cloves, peeled, halved
    and green shoots removed
For the vinegar
  40g/1½oz/3 tbsp granulated sugar
  10ml/2 tsp salt
  5cm/2in piece fresh root ginger,
    peeled and sliced
  15ml/1 tbsp coriander seeds
  2 lemon grass stalks, cut in
    half lengthways
  4 kaffir lime leaves or pared strips of
    lime rind
  600ml/1 pint/2½ cups cider vinegar
  15ml/1 tbsp chopped fresh
    coriander (cilantro)

1 The chillies can be left whole or
halved and seeded. The pickle will be
hotter if you leave the seeds in. If
leaving the chillies whole, prick them
several times with a cocktail stick
(toothpick). Bring a large pan of water
to the boil. Add the chillies, shallots and
garlic. Blanch for 1–2 minutes, then
drain. Rinse all the vegetables under
cold water, then drain again.

2 Prepare the vinegar. Put the sugar,
salt, ginger, coriander seeds, lemon
grass and lime leaves or lime rind in a
pan, pour in the vinegar and bring to
the boil. Reduce the heat to low and
simmer for 3–4 minutes. Leave to cool.

3 Remove and discard the ginger, then
bring the vinegar back to the boil. Add
the fresh coriander, garlic and chillies
and cook for 1 minute.

4 Pack the shallots into sterilized jars,
distributing the lemon grass, lime
leaves, chillies and garlic among them.
Pour over the hot vinegar. Cool, then
seal and store in a cool, dark place for
2 months before eating.

COOK'S TIPS
• Always be careful when making pickles
to be sure that bowls and pans used for
vinegar are non-reactive, that is, they are
not chemically affected by the acid of
the vinegar. China and glass bowls and
stainless steel pans are suitable. Kilner
and Mason jars are ideal containers.
• When packing pickles, make sure that
metal lids will not come in contact with
the pickle. The acid in the vinegar will
corrode the metal. Use plastic-coated or
glass lids with rubber rings. Alternatively,
cover the top of the jar with a circle of
cellophane or waxed paper to prevent
direct contact when using metal lids.
• Take care when handling hot jars. Let
them cool slightly after sterilizing and
before filling to avoid burning yourself.
However, do not let them cool down
completely, or they may crack when the
hot vinegar is poured in.

Energy 135kcal/566kJ; Protein 3.9g; Carbohydrate 30.3g, of which sugars 23.9g; Fat 0.7g, of which saturates 0g, of which polyunsaturates 0.2g; Cholesterol 0mg; Calcium 85mg; Fibre 3.9g; Sodium 12mg.

GREEN PAPAYA SALAD ★

THIS SALAD APPEARS IN MANY GUISES IN SOUTH-EAST ASIA. AS GREEN PAPAYA IS NOT EASY TO GET HOLD OF, FINELY GRATED CARROTS, CUCUMBER OR EVEN CRISP GREEN APPLE CAN BE USED INSTEAD. ALTERNATIVELY, USE VERY THINLY SLICED WHITE CABBAGE.

SERVES FOUR

INGREDIENTS

1 green papaya
4 garlic cloves, coarsely chopped
15ml/1 tbsp chopped shallots
3–4 fresh red chillies, seeded
   and sliced
2.5ml/½ tsp salt
2–3 snake beans or 6 green beans,
   cut into 2cm/¾ in lengths
2 tomatoes, cut into thin wedges
45ml/3 tbsp Thai fish sauce
15ml/1 tbsp caster (superfine) sugar
juice of 1 lime
15ml/1 tbsp crushed roasted peanuts
sliced fresh red chillies, to garnish

1 Cut the papaya in half lengthways. Scrape out the seeds with a spoon and discard, then peel, using a swivel vegetable peeler or a small sharp knife. Shred the flesh finely in a food processor or using a grater.

2 Put the garlic, shallots, red chillies and salt in a large mortar and grind to a paste with a pestle. Add the shredded papaya, a small amount at a time, pounding with the pestle until it becomes slightly limp and soft.

3 Add the sliced snake or green beans and wedges of tomato to the mortar and crush them lightly with the pestle until they are incorporated.

4 Season the mixture with the fish sauce, sugar and lime juice. Transfer the salad to a serving dish and sprinkle with the crushed roasted peanuts. Garnish with the sliced red chillies and serve the salad immediately.

Energy 68kcal/286kJ; Protein 1.3g; Carbohydrate 15.9g, of which sugars 15.6g; Fat 0.3g, of which saturates 0.1g, of which polyunsaturates 0.1g; Cholesterol 0mg; Calcium 37mg; Fibre 3.1g; Sodium 543mg.

GREEN MANGO SALAD ★

ALTHOUGH THE ORANGE AND YELLOW MANGOES AND PAPAYAS ARE DEVOURED IN VAST QUANTITIES WHEN RIPE AND JUICY, THEY ARE ALSO POPULAR WHEN GREEN. THEIR TART FLAVOUR AND CRUNCHY TEXTURE MAKE THEM IDEAL FOR SALADS AND STEWS.

SERVES FOUR

INGREDIENTS
    450g/1lb green mangoes
    grated rind and juice of 2 limes
    30ml/2 tbsp sugar
    30ml/2 tbsp *nuoc mam*
    2 green Thai chillies, seeded and
    finely sliced
    1 small bunch fresh coriander
    (cilantro), stalks removed,
    finely chopped
    salt

1 Peel, halve and stone (pit) the green mangoes, and slice them into thin strips.

2 In a bowl, mix together the lime rind and juice, sugar and *nuoc mam*. Add the mango strips with the chillies and coriander. Add salt to taste and leave to stand for 20 minutes to allow the flavours to mingle before serving.

Energy 69kcal/293kJ; Protein 1.2g; Carbohydrate 16.2g, of which sugars 15.8g; Fat 0.4g, of which saturates 0.1g, of which polyunsaturates 0g; Cholesterol 0mg; Calcium 39mg; Fibre 3.6g; Sodium 7mg.

SWEET AND SOUR SALAD ★

*INDONESIAN ACAR BENING MAKES A PERFECT ACCOMPANIMENT TO A VARIETY OF SPICY DISHES AND
CURRIES, WITH ITS CLEAN TASTE AND BRIGHT, JEWEL-LIKE COLOURS, AND POMEGRANATE SEEDS, THOUGH
NOT TRADITIONAL, MAKE A BEAUTIFUL GARNISH. THIS IS AN ESSENTIAL DISH FOR A BUFFET PARTY.*

SERVES EIGHT

INGREDIENTS
1 small cucumber
1 onion, thinly sliced
1 small, ripe pineapple or 425g/
  15oz can pineapple rings
1 green (bell) pepper, seeded and
  thinly sliced
3 firm tomatoes, chopped
30ml/2 tbsp golden granulated sugar
45–60ml/3–4 tbsp white wine vinegar
120ml/4fl oz/½ cup water
salt
seeds of 1–2 pomegranates,
  to garnish

1 Halve the cucumber lengthways,
remove the seeds, slice and spread on a
plate with the onion. Sprinkle with salt.
After 10 minutes, rinse and dry.

2 If using a fresh pineapple, peel and
core it, removing all the eyes, then cut
it into bitesize pieces. If using canned
pineapple, drain the rings and cut them
into small wedges. Place the pineapple
in a bowl with the cucumber, onion,
green pepper and tomatoes.

3 Heat the sugar, white wine vinegar
and measured water in a pan, stirring
until the sugar has dissolved. Remove
the pan from the heat and leave to
cool. When cold, add a little salt to
taste and pour over the fruit and
vegetables. Cover and chill until
required. Serve in small bowls,
garnished with pomegranate seeds.

VARIATION
To make an Indonesian-style cucumber
salad, salt a salad cucumber as
described in the recipe. Make a half
quantity of the sugar, vinegar and salt
dressing and pour it over the cucumber.
Add a few chopped spring onions
(scallions). Cover and chill. Serve
sprinkled with toasted sesame seeds.

Energy 53kcal/224kJ; Protein 0.9g; Carbohydrate 12.3g, of which sugars 12.1g; Fat 0.3g, of which saturates 0.1g, of which polyunsaturates 0.2g; Cholesterol 0mg; Calcium 20mg; Fibre 1.5g; Sodium 6mg.

THAI FRUIT AND VEGETABLE SALAD ★

THIS FRUIT SALAD IS TRADITIONALLY PRESENTED WITH THE MAIN COURSE AND SERVES AS A COOLER TO COUNTERACT THE HEAT OF THE CHILLIES THAT WILL INEVITABLY BE PRESENT IN THE OTHER DISHES. IT IS A TYPICALLY HARMONIOUS BALANCE OF FLAVOURS.

SERVES SIX

INGREDIENTS
    1 small pineapple
    1 small mango, peeled and sliced
    1 green apple, cored and sliced
    6 rambutans or lychees, peeled and
      stoned (pitted)
    115g/4oz/1 cup green beans,
      trimmed and halved
    1 red onion, sliced
    1 small cucumber, cut into
      short sticks
    115g/4oz/1⅓ cups beansprouts
    2 spring onions (scallions), sliced
    1 ripe tomato, quartered
    225g/8oz cos, romaine or iceberg
      lettuce leaves
For the coconut dipping sauce
    30ml/2 tbsp reduced-fat coconut milk
    30ml/2 tbsp granulated sugar
    75ml/5 tbsp boiling water
    1.5ml/¼ tsp chilli sauce
    15ml/1 tbsp Thai fish sauce
    juice of 1 lime

1 Make the coconut dipping sauce. Spoon the coconut milk, sugar and boiling water into a screw-top jar. Add the chilli and fish sauces and lime juice, close tightly and shake to mix.

2 Trim both ends of the pineapple with a serrated knife, then cut away the outer skin. Remove the central core with an apple corer. Alternatively, quarter the pineapple lengthways and remove the portion of core from each wedge with a knife. Chop the pineapple and set aside with the other fruits.

3 Bring a small pan of lightly salted water to the boil over a medium heat. Add the green beans and cook for 3–4 minutes, until just tender but still retaining some "bite". Drain, refresh under cold running water, drain well again and set aside.

4 To serve, arrange all the fruits and vegetables in small heaps on a platter or in a shallow bowl. Pour the coconut sauce into a small serving bowl and serve separately as a dip.

Energy 100kcal/425kJ; Protein 2.3g; Carbohydrate 22.6g, of which sugars 21.7g; Fat 0.7g, of which saturates 0.1g, of which polyunsaturates 0.3g; Cholesterol 0mg; Calcium 50mg; Fibre 3.2g; Sodium 190mg.

SOYA BEANSPROUT HERB SALAD ★

HIGH IN PROTEIN AND FAT, SOYA BEANSPROUTS ARE PARTICULARLY FAVOURED IN CAMBODIA. UNLIKE MUNG BEANSPROUTS, THEY ARE SLIGHTLY POISONOUS WHEN RAW AND NEED TO BE PARBOILED BEFORE USING. TOSSED IN A SALAD, THEY ARE OFTEN EATEN WITH NOODLES AND RICE.

2 Bring a pan of salted water to the boil. Drop in the beansprouts and blanch for a minute only. Drain and refresh under cold water until cool. Drain again and put them into a clean dish towel. Shake out the excess water.

3 Put the beansprouts into a bowl with the spring onions. Pour over the dressing and toss well. Garnish with coriander leaves and serve.

SERVES FOUR

INGREDIENTS
    450g/1lb fresh soya beansprouts
    2 spring onions (scallions), finely
      sliced
    1 small bunch fresh coriander
      (cilantro), stalks removed
For the dressing
    5ml/1 tsp sesame oil
    30ml/2 tbsp *tuk trey*
    15ml/1 tbsp white rice vinegar
    10ml/2 tsp palm sugar
    1 red chilli, seeded and
      finely sliced
    15g/½oz fresh young root ginger,
      finely shredded

1 First make the dressing. In a bowl, beat the oil, *tuk trey* and rice vinegar with the sugar, until it dissolves. Stir in the chilli and ginger and leave to stand for 30 minutes to allow the flavours to develop.

Energy 58kcal/245kJ; Protein 3.8g; Carbohydrate 7.9g, of which sugars 5.8g; Fat 1.5g, of which saturates 0.2g, of which polyunsaturates 0.6g; Cholesterol 0mg; Calcium 52mg; Fibre 2.5g; Sodium 11mg

VIETNAMESE TABLE SALAD ★

*WHEN THIS VIETNAMESE TABLE SALAD IS SERVED ON ITS OWN, THE VEGETABLES AND FRUIT ARE
USUALLY FOLDED INTO LITTLE PACKETS USING LETTUCE LEAVES OR RICE WRAPPERS, AND THEN
DIPPED IN A SAUCE, OR ADDED BIT BY BIT TO BOWLS OF RICE OR NOODLES.*

SERVES SIX

INGREDIENTS
    half a cucumber, peeled and sliced
    200g/7oz/scant 1 cup beansprouts
    2 carrots, peeled and finely sliced
    2 unripe star fruit (carambola),
      finely sliced
    2 green bananas, finely sliced
    1 firm papaya, cut in half, seeds
      removed, peeled and finely sliced
    1 bunch each fresh mint and basil,
      stalks removed
    1 crunchy lettuce, leaves separated
    juice of 1 lime
    dipping sauce, to serve

1 Arrange the cucumber, beansprouts, carrots, star fruit, green bananas, papaya, mint and basil attractively on a large plate. Place the lettuce leaves on one side so that they can be used as wrappers.

2 Squeeze the lime juice over the sliced fruits, particularly the bananas to help them retain their colour, and place the salad in the middle of the table. Serve with a dipping sauce.

Energy 94kcal/397kJ; Protein 2.5g; Carbohydrate 20.6g, of which sugars 11.6g; Fat 0.7g, of which saturates 0.1g, of which polyunsaturates 0.3g; Cholesterol 0mg; Calcium 61mg; Fibre 3.4g; Sodium 14mg.

SWEET-AND-SOUR CUCUMBER WITH CHILLIES, CORIANDER AND MINT ★

SHORT, FAT CUCUMBERS ARE A COMMON SIGHT IN THE MARKETS THROUGHOUT SOUTH-EAST ASIA. THIS SALAD IS A GREAT ADDITION TO A SUMMER BARBECUE OR THE SALAD TABLE, AND IS A DELIGHTFUL ACCOMPANIMENT TO ANY MEAT, POULTRY AND SEAFOOD DISHES.

SERVES SIX

INGREDIENTS

2 cucumbers
30ml/2 tbsp sugar
100ml/3½fl oz/½ cup rice vinegar
juice of half a lime
2 green Thai chillies, seeded and
  finely sliced
2 shallots, halved and finely sliced
1 small bunch each fresh coriander
  (cilantro) and mint, stalks removed,
  leaves finely chopped
salt
fresh coriander leaves, to garnish

COOK'S TIP
Decorate the dish with edible flowers,
such as nasturtiums, to add colour.

1 Use a vegetable peeler to remove strips of the cucumber peel. Halve the cucumbers lengthways and cut into slices. Place the slices on a plate and sprinkle with a little salt. Leave them to stand for 15 minutes. Rinse well, drain the slices and pat them dry with kitchen paper.

2 In a bowl, mix the sugar with the vinegar until it has dissolved, then stir in the lime juice and a little salt to taste.

3 Add the chillies, shallots, herbs and cucumber to the dressing and leave to stand for 15–20 minutes. Garnish with coriander leaves and a flower, if you like.

Energy 33kcal/138kJ; Protein 0.9g; Carbohydrate 7.2g, of which sugars 6.9g; Fat 0.2g, of which saturates 0g, of which polyunsaturates 0g; Cholesterol 0mg; Calcium 34mg; Fibre 1g; Sodium 5mg.

LOTUS STEM SALAD WITH SHALLOTS AND SHREDDED FRESH BASIL ★

YOU MAY BE LUCKY ENOUGH TO FIND FRESH LOTUS STEMS IN AN ASIAN MARKET, OR, AS HERE, YOU CAN USE THE ONES PRESERVED IN BRINE. ALTERNATIVELY, TRY THIS RECIPE WITH FRESHLY STEAMED, CRUNCHY ASPARAGUS TIPS FOR A LOW-FAT RECIPE THAT TASTES DELICIOUS.

SERVES FOUR

INGREDIENTS
half a cucumber
225g/8oz jar preserved lotus
   stems, drained and cut into
   5cm/2in strips
2 shallots, finely sliced
25g/1oz/½ cup fresh basil
   leaves, shredded
salt
fresh coriander (cilantro) leaves,
   to garnish
For the dressing
juice of 1 lime
30ml/2 tbsp *nuoc mam*
1 red Thai chilli, seeded
   and chopped
1 garlic clove, crushed
15ml/1 tbsp sugar

1 To make the dressing, mix together the dressing ingredients in a bowl and set aside.

2 Peel the cucumber and cut it into 5cm/2in batons. Soak the batons in cold salted water for 20 minutes. Put the lotus stems into a bowl of water. Using a pair of chopsticks, stir the water so that the loose fibres of the stems wrap around the sticks.

VARIATION
Try this recipe with freshly steamed, crunchy asparagus tips instead of lotus stems for a healthy and delicious, low-fat, low-cholesterol recipe.

3 Drain the stems and put them in a bowl. Drain the cucumber batons and add to the bowl, then add the shallots, shredded basil leaves and the prepared dressing. Leave the salad to marinate for 20 minutes before serving. Garnish with fresh coriander leaves.

COOK'S TIP
If you cannot find the stems, fresh lotus roots make a good substitute and are readily available in Asian markets. They grow in sausage-like links, each one about 18–23cm/7–9in long. Once the mud that coats them has been washed off, a pale beige-pink skin is revealed. When buying fresh lotus roots, choose ones that feel heavy for their size, as this is an indication that they are full of liquid. This means that the roots will absorb the flavours of the dressing while retaining a crunchy texture. They should be peeled and soaked in water with a little lemon juice before being added to the salad, to retain their pale colour.

Energy 40kcal/168kJ; Protein 1.4g; Carbohydrate 8.3g, of which sugars 7.5g; Fat 0.3g, of which saturates 0g, of which polyunsaturates 0.1g; Cholesterol 0mg; Calcium 55mg; Fibre 1.7g; Sodium 573mg.

AUBERGINE SALAD ★

AN APPETIZING AND UNUSUAL SALAD THAT YOU WILL FIND YOURSELF MAKING OVER AND OVER AGAIN.
ROASTING THE AUBERGINES REALLY BRINGS OUT THEIR FLAVOUR.

SERVES SIX

INGREDIENTS

2 aubergines (eggplant)
15ml/1 tbsp sunflower oil
30ml/2 tbsp dried shrimp, soaked in
 warm water for 10 minutes
15ml/1 tbsp coarsely chopped garlic
1 hard-boiled egg, chopped
4 shallots, thinly sliced
 into rings
fresh coriander (cilantro) leaves and
 2 fresh red chillies, seeded and
 sliced, to garnish
For the dressing
 30ml/2 tbsp fresh lime juice
 5ml/1 tsp palm sugar or light
 muscovado (brown) sugar
 30ml/2 tbsp Thai fish sauce

1 Preheat the grill (broiler) to medium or preheat the oven to 180°C/350°F/ Gas 4. Prick the aubergines several times with a skewer, then arrange on a baking sheet. Cook them under the grill for 30–40 minutes, or until they are charred and tender. Alternatively, roast them by placing them directly on the shelf of the oven for about 1 hour, turning them at least twice. Remove the aubergines and set aside until they are cool enough to handle.

2 Meanwhile, make the dressing. Put the lime juice, palm or muscovado sugar and fish sauce into a small bowl. Whisk well with a fork or balloon whisk. Cover with clear film (plastic wrap) and set aside until required.

3 When the aubergines are cool enough to handle, peel off the skin and cut the flesh into medium slices.

4 Heat the oil in a small frying pan. Drain the dried shrimp thoroughly and add them to the pan with the garlic. Cook over a medium heat for about 3 minutes, until golden. Remove from the pan and set aside.

5 Arrange the aubergine slices on a serving dish. Top with the hard-boiled egg, shallots and dried shrimp mixture. Drizzle over the dressing and garnish with the coriander and red chillies.

VARIATION
For a special occasion, use salted duck's or quail's eggs, cut in half, instead of chopped hen's eggs.

Energy 61kcal/254kJ; Protein 4.8g; Carbohydrate 3.6g, of which sugars 2.8g; Fat 3.2g, of which saturates 0.6g, of which polyunsaturates 1.5g; Cholesterol 57mg; Calcium 75mg; Fibre 1.6g; Sodium 408mg.

CABBAGE SALAD ★

THIS IS A SIMPLE AND DELICIOUS WAY OF SERVING A SOMEWHAT MUNDANE VEGETABLE. CLASSIC THAI
FLAVOURS OF CHILLI AND PEANUTS PERMEATE THIS COLOURFUL WARM SALAD.

SERVES SIX

INGREDIENTS
   15ml/1 tbsp sunflower oil
   2 large fresh red chillies, seeded
     and cut into thin strips
   6 garlic cloves, thinly sliced
   6 shallots, thinly sliced
   1 small cabbage, shredded
   15ml/1 tbsp coarsely chopped
     roasted peanuts, to garnish
For the dressing
   30ml/2 tbsp Thai fish sauce
   grated rind of 1 lime
   30ml/2 tbsp fresh lime juice
   120ml/4fl oz/½ cup reduced-fat
     coconut milk

VARIATION
Cauliflower and broccoli can also be
cooked in this way.

1 Make the dressing by mixing the fish
sauce, lime rind and juice and coconut
milk in a bowl. Whisk until thoroughly
combined, then set aside.

2 Heat the oil in a wok. Stir-fry the
chillies, garlic and shallots over a
medium heat for 3–4 minutes, until the
shallots are brown and crisp. Remove
with a slotted spoon and set aside.

3 Bring a large pan of lightly salted
water to the boil. Add the cabbage and
blanch for 2–3 minutes. Tip it into a
colander, drain well and put into a bowl.

4 Whisk the dressing again, add it to
the warm cabbage and toss to mix.
Transfer the salad to a serving dish.
Sprinkle with the fried shallot mixture
and the peanuts. Serve immediately.

Energy 70kcal/290kJ; Protein 2.2g; Carbohydrate 8.3g, of which sugars 7g; Fat 3.3g, of which saturates 0.5g, of which polyunsaturates 1.6g; Cholesterol 0mg; Calcium 51mg; Fibre 2.2g; Sodium 206mg.

POMELO AND CRAB SALAD ★

TYPICALLY, A THAI MEAL INCLUDES A SELECTION OF ABOUT FIVE DISHES, ONE OF WHICH IS OFTEN A
REFRESHING AND PALATE-CLEANSING SALAD THAT FEATURES TROPICAL FRUIT.

SERVES SIX

INGREDIENTS
  15ml/1 tbsp sunflower oil
  4 shallots, finely sliced
  2 garlic cloves, finely sliced
  1 large pomelo
  15ml/1 tbsp roasted peanuts
  115g/4oz cooked peeled
    prawns (shrimp)
  115g/4oz cooked crab meat
  10–12 small fresh mint leaves
For the dressing
  30ml/2 tbsp Thai fish sauce
  15ml/1 tbsp palm sugar or light
    muscovado (brown) sugar
  30ml/2 tbsp fresh lime juice
For the garnish
  2 spring onions (scallions),
    thinly sliced
  2 fresh red chillies, seeded and
    thinly sliced
  fresh coriander (cilantro) leaves
  shredded fresh coconut (optional)

1 Make the dressing. Mix the fish sauce, sugar and lime juice in a bowl. Whisk well, then cover with clear film (plastic wrap) and set aside.

2 Heat the oil in a small frying pan, add the shallots and garlic and cook over a medium heat until they are golden. Remove from the pan and set aside.

3 Peel the pomelo and break the flesh into small pieces, taking care to remove any membranes.

4 Grind the peanuts coarsely and put them in a salad bowl. Add the pomelo flesh, prawns, crab meat, mint leaves and the shallot mixture. Pour over the dressing, toss lightly and sprinkle with the spring onions, chillies and coriander leaves. Add the shredded coconut, if using. Serve immediately.

COOK'S TIP
The pomelo is a large citrus fruit that looks rather like a grapefruit, although it is not, as is sometimes thought, a hybrid. It is slightly pear-shaped with thick, yellow, dimpled skin and pinkish-yellow flesh that is both sturdier and drier than that of a grapefruit. It also has a sharper taste. Pomelos are sometimes known as "shaddocks" after the sea captain who brought them from their native Polynesia to the Caribbean.

Energy 71kcal/300kJ; Protein 8g; Carbohydrate 5.8g, of which sugars 5.4g; Fat 2g, of which saturates 0.3g, of which polyunsaturates 0.7g; Cholesterol 51mg; Calcium 53mg; Fibre 0.8g; Sodium 144mg.

SEAFOOD SALAD WITH FRAGRANT HERBS ★★

THIS IS A SPECTACULAR SALAD. THE LUSCIOUS COMBINATION OF PRAWNS, SCALLOPS AND SQUID, MAKES IT THE IDEAL CHOICE FOR A SPECIAL CELEBRATION.

SERVES FOUR TO SIX

INGREDIENTS

250ml/8fl oz/1 cup fish stock
   or water
350g/12oz squid, cleaned and cut
   into rings
12 raw king prawns (jumbo shrimp),
   peeled, with tails intact
12 scallops
50g/2oz cellophane noodles, soaked
   in warm water for 30 minutes
½ cucumber, cut into thin batons
1 lemon grass stalk, finely chopped
2 kaffir lime leaves, finely shredded
2 shallots, thinly sliced
30ml/2 tbsp chopped spring
   onions (scallions)
30ml/2 tbsp fresh coriander
   (cilantro) leaves
12–15 fresh mint leaves,
   coarsely torn
4 fresh red chillies, seeded and cut
   into slivers
juice of 1–2 limes
30ml/2 tbsp Thai fish sauce
fresh coriander sprigs, to garnish

1 Pour the fish stock or water into a medium pan, set over a high heat and bring to the boil. Cook each type of seafood separately in the stock for 3–4 minutes. Remove with a slotted spoon and set aside to cool.

2 Drain the noodles. Using scissors, cut them into short lengths, about 5cm/2in long. Place them in a serving bowl and add the cucumber, lemon grass, kaffir lime leaves, shallots, spring onions, coriander, mint and chillies.

3 Pour over the lime juice and fish sauce. Mix well, then add the seafood. Toss lightly. Garnish with the fresh coriander sprigs and serve.

Energy 339kcal/1420kJ; Protein 27.3g; Carbohydrate 42g, of which sugars 2.3g; Fat 6.8g, of which saturates 0.9g, of which polyunsaturates 3.2g; Cholesterol 219mg; Calcium 148mg; Fibre 1.7g; Sodium 861mg

THAI PRAWN SALAD <u>WITH</u> GARLIC DRESSING <u>AND</u> FRIZZLED SHALLOTS ★

IN THIS INTENSELY FLAVOURED SALAD, SWEET PRAWNS AND MANGO ARE PARTNERED WITH A SWEET-SOUR GARLIC DRESSING HEIGHTENED WITH THE HOT TASTE OF CHILLI. THE CRISP FRIZZLED SHALLOTS ARE A TRADITIONAL ADDITION TO THAI SALADS.

SERVES SIX

INGREDIENTS

675g/1½lb medium raw prawns
(shrimp), peeled and deveined,
with tails intact
finely shredded rind of 1 lime
½ fresh red chilli, seeded and
finely chopped
15ml/1 tbsp olive oil, plus extra
for spraying
1 ripe but firm mango
2 carrots, cut into long thin shreds
10cm/4in piece cucumber, sliced
1 small red onion, halved and
thinly sliced
a few fresh mint sprigs
a few fresh coriander (cilantro) sprigs
15ml/1 tbsp roasted peanuts,
coarsely chopped
4 large shallots, thinly sliced and
fried until crisp in 5ml/1 tsp
sunflower oil
salt and ground black pepper
For the dressing
1 large garlic clove, chopped
10–15ml/2–3 tsp caster
(superfine) sugar
juice of 2 limes
15–30ml/1–2 tbsp Thai fish sauce
1 fresh red chilli, seeded and
finely chopped
5–10ml/1–2 tsp light rice vinegar

1 Place the prawns in a glass dish with the lime rind, chilli, oil and seasoning. Toss to mix and leave to marinate at room temperature for 30–40 minutes.

2 Make the dressing. Place the garlic in a mortar with 10ml/2 tsp of the caster sugar. Pound with a pestle until smooth, then work in about three-quarters of the lime juice, followed by 15ml/1 tbsp of the Thai fish sauce.

3 Transfer the dressing to a jug (pitcher). Stir in half the chopped red chilli. Taste the dressing and add more sugar, lime juice and/or fish sauce, if you think they are necessary, and stir in light rice vinegar to taste.

4 Peel and stone (pit) the mango. The best way to do this is to cut either side of the large central stone (pit), as close to it as possible, with a sharp knife. Cut the flesh into very fine strips and cut off any flesh still adhering to the stone.

5 Place the strips of mango in a bowl and add the carrots, cucumber slices and red onion. Pour over about half the dressing and toss thoroughly. Arrange the salad on four to six individual serving plates or in bowls.

6 Heat a ridged, cast-iron griddle pan or heavy frying pan until very hot. Spray with a little oil, then sear the marinated prawns for 2–3 minutes on each side, until they turn pink and are patched with brown on the outside. Arrange the prawns on the salads.

7 Sprinkle the remaining dressing over the salads and garnish with the mint and coriander sprigs. Sprinkle over the remaining chilli with the peanuts and crisp-fried shallots. Serve immediately.

COOK'S TIP
To devein the prawns (shrimp), make a shallow cut down the back of each prawn, using a small, sharp knife. Using the tip of the knife, lift out the thin, black vein, then rinse the prawn thoroughly under cold, running water, drain it and pat it dry with kitchen paper.

Energy 156kcal/656kJ; Protein 20.9g; Carbohydrate 8.9g, of which sugars 8.4g; Fat 4.3g, of which saturates 0.7g, of which polyunsaturates 1g; Cholesterol 219mg; Calcium 102mg; Fibre 1.4g; Sodium 397mg.

TROPICAL FRUIT GRATIN ★★

THIS OUT-OF-THE-ORDINARY GRATIN IS STRICTLY FOR GROWN-UPS. A COLOURFUL COMBINATION OF FRUIT IS TOPPED WITH A SIMPLE SABAYON BEFORE BEING FLASHED UNDER THE GRILL.

SERVES FOUR

INGREDIENTS
2 tamarillos
½ sweet pineapple
1 ripe mango
175g/6oz/1½ cups blackberries
120ml/4fl oz/½ cup sparkling
  white wine
115g/4oz/½ cup caster
  (superfine) sugar
6 egg yolks

VARIATION
Boiling drives off the alcohol in the wine, but children do not always appreciate the flavour. Substitute orange juice if making the gratin for them. White grape juice or pineapple juice would also work well.

1 Cut each tamarillo in half lengthways, then into thick slices. Cut the rind and core from the pineapple and take spiral slices off the outside to remove the eyes. Cut the flesh into chunks. Peel the mango, cut it in half and cut the flesh from the stone (pit) in slices.

2 Divide all the fruit, including the blackberries, among four 14cm/5½in gratin dishes set on a baking sheet and set aside. Heat the wine and sugar in a pan until the sugar has dissolved. Bring to the boil and cook for 5 minutes.

3 Put the egg yolks in a large heatproof bowl. Place the bowl over a pan of simmering water and whisk until pale. Slowly pour on the hot sugar syrup, whisking all the time, until the mixture thickens. Preheat the grill (broiler).

4 Spoon the mixture over the fruit. Place the baking sheet holding the dishes on a low shelf under the hot grill until the topping is golden. Serve the gratin hot.

GRILLED PINEAPPLE WITH PAPAYA SAUCE ★

PINEAPPLE AND STEM GINGER IS A CLASSIC COMBINATION. WHEN COOKED IN THIS WAY, THE FRUIT TAKES ON A SUPERB FLAVOUR AND IS SIMPLY SENSATIONAL WHEN SERVED WITH THE PAPAYA SAUCE.

SERVES SIX

INGREDIENTS
1 sweet pineapple
melted butter, for greasing
  and brushing
2 pieces drained stem ginger in
  syrup, cut into fine matchsticks,
  plus 30ml/2 tbsp of the syrup
  from the jar
30ml/2 tbsp demerara (raw) sugar
pinch of ground cinnamon
fresh mint sprigs, to decorate
For the sauce
1 ripe papaya, peeled and seeded
175ml/6fl oz/¾ cup apple juice

1 Peel the pineapple and take spiral slices off the outside to remove the eyes. Cut it crossways into six slices, each 2.5cm/1in thick. Line a baking sheet with a sheet of foil, rolling up the sides to make a rim. Grease the foil with melted butter. Preheat the grill (broiler).

2 Arrange the pineapple slices on the lined baking sheet. Brush with butter, then top with the ginger matchsticks, sugar and cinnamon. Drizzle over the stem ginger syrup. Grill (broil) for 5–7 minutes or until the slices are golden and lightly charred on top.

3 Meanwhile, make the sauce. Cut a few slices from the papaya and set aside, then purée the rest with the apple juice in a blender or food processor.

4 Press the purée through a sieve placed over a bowl, then stir in any juices from cooking the pineapple. Serve the pineapple slices with a little sauce drizzled around each plate. Decorate with the reserved papaya slices and the mint sprigs.

COOK'S TIP
Try the papaya sauce with savoury dishes, too. It tastes great with grilled chicken and game birds as well as pork and lamb.

Top: Energy 300kcal/1270kJ; Protein 6.2g; Carbohydrate 52.8g, of which sugars 52.7g; Fat 8.7g, of which saturates 2.4g, of which polyunsaturates 1.1g; Cholesterol 302mg; Calcium 119mg; Fibre 4.6g; Sodium 22mg.
Bottom: Energy 97kcal/415kJ; Protein 0.7g; Carbohydrate 24.7g, of which sugars 24.7g; Fat 0.2g, of which saturates 0g, of which polyunsaturates 0.1g; Cholesterol 0mg; Calcium 33mg; Fibre 2.3g; Sodium 19mg.

STEWED PUMPKIN IN COCONUT CREAM ★

FRUIT STEWED IN COCONUT MILK IS A POPULAR DESSERT IN THAILAND. PUMPKINS, BANANAS AND MELONS CAN ALL BE PREPARED IN THIS SIMPLE BUT TASTY WAY.

SERVES FOUR TO SIX

INGREDIENTS
1kg/2¼lb kabocha pumpkin
750ml/1¼ pints/3 cups reduced-fat
  coconut milk
175g/6oz/¾ cup granulated sugar
pinch of salt
4–6 fresh mint sprigs, to decorate

COOK'S TIP
To make the decoration, wash the pumpkin seeds to remove any fibres, then pat them dry on kitchen paper. Roast them in a dry frying pan, or spread them out on a baking sheet and grill (broil) until golden brown, tossing them frequently to prevent them from burning.

1 Cut the pumpkin in half using a large, sharp knife, then cut away and discard the skin. Scoop out the seed cluster. Reserve a few seeds and throw away the rest. Using a sharp knife, cut the pumpkin flesh into pieces that are about 5cm/2in long and 2cm/¾in thick.

2 Pour the coconut milk into a pan. Add the sugar and salt and bring to the boil. Add the pumpkin and simmer for about 10–15 minutes, until it is tender. Serve warm, in individual dishes. Decorate each serving with a mint sprig and toasted pumpkin seeds (see Cook's Tip).

MANGOES WITH STICKY RICE ★

STICKY RICE IS JUST AS GOOD IN DESSERTS AS IN SAVOURY DISHES, AND RIPE MANGOES, WITH THEIR DELICATE FRAGRANCE AND VELVETY FLESH, COMPLEMENT IT ESPECIALLY WELL.

SERVES FOUR

INGREDIENTS
115g/4oz/⅔ cup white
  glutinous rice
175ml/6fl oz/¾ cup reduced-fat
  coconut milk
45ml/3 tbsp granulated sugar
pinch of salt
2 ripe mangoes
strips of pared lime rind,
  to decorate

1 Rinse the glutinous rice thoroughly in several changes of cold water, then leave to soak overnight in a bowl of fresh cold water.

COOK'S TIP
Like dairy cream, the thickest and richest part of coconut milk always rises to the top. Whenever you open a can or carton, spoon off this top layer and use the thinner, lower fat bottom layer in cooking.

2 Drain the rice well and spread it out evenly in a steamer lined with muslin or cheesecloth. Cover and steam over a pan of simmering water for about 20 minutes, or until the rice is tender.

3 Reserve 45ml/3 tbsp of the cream from the top of the coconut milk. Pour the remainder into a pan and add the sugar and salt. Heat, stirring constantly, until the sugar has dissolved, then bring to the boil. Remove the pan from the heat, pour the coconut milk into a bowl and leave to cool.

4 Tip the cooked rice into a bowl and pour over the cooled coconut milk mixture. Stir well, then leave the rice mixture to stand for 10–15 minutes.

5 Meanwhile, peel the mangoes, cut the flesh away from the central stones (pits) and cut into slices.

6 Spoon the rice on to individual serving plates. Arrange the mango slices on one side, then drizzle with the reserved coconut cream. Decorate with strips of lime rind and serve.

Top: Energy 164kcal/701kJ; Protein 1.7g; Carbohydrate 40.3g, of which sugars 39.4g; Fat 0.7g, of which saturates 0.4g, of which polyunsaturates 0g; Cholesterol 0mg; Calcium 100mg; Fibre 1.7g; Sodium 139mg.
Bottom: Energy 200kcal/846kJ; Protein 3.1g; Carbohydrate 46g, of which sugars 24.3g; Fat 0.8g, of which saturates 0.2g, of which polyunsaturates 0g; Cholesterol 0mg; Calcium 32mg; Fibre 2g; Sodium 51mg.

CHURROS ★

THESE IRRESISTIBLE FRITTERS, SERVED AT EVERY OPPORTUNITY WITH HOT CHOCOLATE OR COFFEE, CAME TO THE PHILIPPINES WITH THE SPANISH WHO WERE KEEN TO KEEP MEMORIES OF HOME ALIVE.

MAKES ABOUT TWENTY-FOUR

INGREDIENTS
450ml/15fl oz/scant 2 cups water
15ml/1 tbsp olive oil
15ml/1 tbsp sugar, plus extra
for sprinkling
2.5ml/¹/₂ tsp salt
150g/5oz/1¹/₄ cups plain
(all-purpose) flour
1 large (US extra large) egg
sunflower oil, for deep-frying
caster (superfine) sugar,
for sprinkling

COOK'S TIP
If you don't have a piping (pastry) bag, you could fry teaspoons of mixture in the same way. Don't try to fry too many churros at a time as they swell a little during cooking.

1 Mix the water, oil, sugar and salt in a large pan and bring to the boil. Remove from the heat, and then sift in the flour. Beat well with a wooden spoon until smooth.

2 Beat in the egg to make a smooth, glossy mixture with a piping consistency. Spoon into a piping (pastry) bag fitted with a large star nozzle.

3 Heat the oil in a wok or deep fryer to 190°C/375°F. Pipe loops of the mixture, two at a time, into the hot oil. Cook the loops for 3–4 minutes until they are golden.

4 Lift out the churros with a wire skimmer or slotted spoon and drain them on kitchen paper. Dredge them with caster sugar and serve warm.

LECHE FLAN ★

SERVE THIS TRADITIONAL DESSERT HOT OR COLD WITH CHILLED YOGURT. THE USE OF EVAPORATED MILK REFLECTS THE 50 YEARS OF AMERICAN PRESENCE IN THE PHILIPPINES.

SERVES EIGHT

INGREDIENTS
5 large eggs
30ml/2 tbsp caster (superfine) sugar
few drops vanilla extract
410g/14¹/₂oz can reduced-fat
evaporated (unsweetened
condensed) milk
300ml/¹/₂ pint/1¹/₄ cups skimmed milk
5ml/1 tsp finely grated lime rind
strips of lime rind, to decorate
For the caramel
225g/8oz/1 cup sugar
120ml/4fl oz/¹/₂ cup water

1 Make the caramel. Put the sugar and water in a heavy pan. Stir to dissolve the sugar, then boil without stirring until golden. Pour into eight ramekins, rotating to coat the sides.

2 Preheat the oven to 150°C/300°F/ Gas 2. Beat the eggs, sugar and vanilla extract in a bowl. Mix the evaporated milk and fresh milk in a pan. Heat to just below boiling point, then pour on to the egg mixture, stirring all the time. Strain the custard mixture into a jug, add the grated lime rind and cool. Pour into the caramel-coated ramekins.

3 Place the ramekins in a roasting pan and pour in enough warm water to come halfway up the sides of the dishes.

4 Transfer the roasting pan to the oven and cook the custards for 35–45 minutes or until they just shimmer when the ramekins are gently shaken.

5 Serve the custards in their ramekin dishes or by inverting on to serving plates, in which case break the caramel and use as decoration. The custards can be served warm or cold, decorated with strips of lime rind.

COOK'S TIP
Make extra caramel, if you like, for a garnish. Pour on to lightly oiled foil and leave to set, then crush with a rolling pin.

Top: Energy 62kcal/257kJ; Protein 0.9g; Carbohydrate 5.7g, of which sugars 0.9g; Fat 4.1g, of which saturates 0.5g, of which polyunsaturates 2.2g; Cholesterol 8mg; Calcium 10mg; Fibre 0.2g; Sodium 3mg.
Bottom: Energy 320kcal/1361kJ; Protein 10.5g; Carbohydrate 65.7g, of which sugars 65.7g; Fat 3.7g, of which saturates 1.1g, of which polyunsaturates 0.4g; Cholesterol 121mg; Calcium 250mg; Fibre 0g; Sodium 139mg.

GLOSSARY

Aduki beans Small, brownish red beans that are often used in sweet recipes.

Agar-agar A gelling and setting agent made from seaweed.

Asian pear One of several varieties of pears with green, russet or yellow skin.

Balachan The Malay term for shrimp paste. An essential ingredient in a wide variety of South East Asian dishes, it is made from tiny shrimps which have been salted, dried and pounded and then left to ferment in hot humid conditions.

Choi sum A mild-tasting brassica.

Chow chow A relish made from pickled vegetables.

Coconut cream A thick cream made from coconut milk

Coconut milk A milk made by soaking grated coconut flesh in hot water and then squeezing it to extract the liquid.

Fermented rice A popular sweetmeat made from fermented cooked glutinous rice.

Galangal Similar to fresh ginger, galangal is a rhizome. The finger-like protruberances of galangal tend to be thinner and paler in colour but the two look similar and are used in much the same way.

Glutinous rice Often referred to as sweet or sticky rice, glutinous rice comes in two varieties, black and white. The grains clump together when cooked.

Above: Thai aubergines are usually small and fairly round in shape.

Hakusai (Chinese cabbage) A vegetable with white stem and green leaves.

Holy basil A pungent variety of basil also known as hot basil.

Jasmine rice A long-grain rice, also known as fragrant or scented rice, with a slightly nutty flavour.

Kabocha A squash with dark green skin and yellow flesh, and a nutty flavour.

Below: Black and white glutinous rice.

Kaffir lime leaves The leaves of an inedible fruit that impart a distinctive citrus flavour to soups, curries, fish and chicken dishes. The rind is also used in some recipes.

Kapi The Thai term for shrimp paste. An essential ingredient in a wide variety of South-east Asian dishes, it is made from tiny shrimps which have been salted, dried and pounded and then left to ferment in hot humid conditions.

Kroeung A Cambodian herb paste made from a blend of lemon grass, galangal, garlic and turmeric.

Lemon basil A variety of basil grown in Thailand used in soups and salads.

Long beans The immature pods of black-eyed beans (peas), also referred to as snake beans.

Lotus root A white-fleshed root from the lotus plant.

Mooli (Daikon) A long, white vegetable of the radish family.

Mung beans A small bean, much used in Vietnam and Cambodia.

Nam pla The Thai term for fish sauce, an essential flavouring in a vast range of savoury dishes.

Nam prik A general term for pungent and hot sauces or dips.

Ngapi The Burmese term for shrimp paste. An essential ingredient in a wide variety of South-east Asian dishes, it is made from tiny shrimps which have been salted, dried and pounded and then left to ferment in hot humid conditions.

Nuoc cham A popular Vietnamese dipping sauce made from chillies.

Nuoc mam The Vietnamese term for fish sauce, an essential flavouring in a vast range of savoury dishes.

Pak choi (bok choy) Loose-leafed brassica with white stems.

Rice flour A flour made by grinding the raw grain to a very fine powder.

Rice sticks These flat, thin dried rice noodles resemble linguine and are available in several widths.

Shimeji Meaty-textured mushroom, similar to oyster mushrooms.

Shiitaki A variety of fungus with a brown cap and white stem.

Sod prik A hot and spicy chilli sauce, originally from China but now popular in Thailand and Vietnam.

Right: Taro is a rough-skinned tuber.

Right: Yam beans look like large brown turnips and are good with spicy dips.

Tamarind A tart and sour ingredient from the fruit pods of the tamarind tree which is made into a paste or sold in blocks. Tamarind imparts a fruity and refreshing flavour to savoury dishes.

Taro A starchy tuber that tastes rather like a potato.

Terasi The Indonesian term for shrimp paste. It is made from tiny shrimps which have been salted, dried and pounded and then left to ferment in hot humid conditions.

Thai basil A herb with an anise flavour.

Star anise A star-shaped spice closely resembling anise in flavour.

Star fruit Also known as carambola, this is a bright yellow fruit with a bland, slightly sharp flavour.

Straw mushrooms Delicate, sweet and the most popular variety in Thai cooking.

Toasted rice flour A speciality of Vietnamese cooking with a coarse texture and a smoky flavour.

Tree ear A dried fungi with a crunchy, chewy texture.

Tuk prahoc The Cambodian term for fish sauce, an essential flavouring in a vast range of savoury dishes.

Tuk trey A Cambodian fish sauce mae by fermenting small fish and salt layered in wooden barrels.

Wood ear A dried fungi, also known as cloud ears, with a woody aroma.

MAP OF SOUTH-EAST ASIA

The food of Thailand and South-east Asia is a joy to the senses, combining the refreshing aroma of kaffir lime leaves with the pungency of brilliant red chillies and ginger and the magical flavours of coconut and fresh basil. Throughout the region, the emphasis is on good, freshly cooked food, and every recipe here has been specially adapted for today's low-fat diet.

Rice is the staple diet of the whole region, cultivated in South-east Asia for over five thousand years. Fish forms an important part of the diet in nearly every country from Vietnam and the Philippines to the 13,000 islands of Indonesia. The famous red, yellow and green curries of Thailand are quick and easy to prepare, using reduced-fat coconut milk. Southern India and China influenced Malaysian cooking, and samosas exist side-by side with beef rendang. Ingredients such as lemon grass and galangal are now available worldwide, meaning there has never been a better time to explore Thai and South-east Asian cooking.

Right: Asia is a vast region, from China, Japan and Korea, to Thailand, Vietnam and the South-east Asian islands of Malaysia, Indonesia and the Philippines.

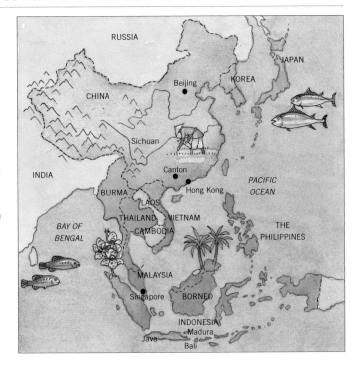

H
herbs 72, 190
  pan-steamed mussels with
    lemon grass, chilli and
    Thai herbs 70
  rice noodles with fresh
    herbs 190
honey 168, 233
hot and fragrant trout 124
hot and sour prawn soup 46–7
hot and sour soup 53
hot and sweet vegetable and
  tofu soup 34
hot Thai pickled shallots 211

I
ice cream
  coconut ice cream 230
Indonesian coconut rice 179

J
jaggery *see* palm sugar
jasmine flower syrup and
  papayas 234
jasmine rice with prawns and
  Thai basil 184
jungle curry 97
jungle curry of guinea fowl 144
jungle fruits in lemon grass
  syrup 235

K
kaffir lime 85
kumquats 16

L
lamb 23
  lamb saté 153
larp of Chiang Mai 170–1
leche flan 248–9
lemon grass 17, 111, 202
  brown rice with lime and
    lemon grass 183
  chicken and lemon grass
    curry 141
  chicken rice soup with lemon
    grass 48–9
  chicken with chillies and
    lemon grass 135
  grilled prawns with lemon
    grass 73
  jungle fruits in lemon grass
    syrup 235

lemon grass pork 159
lemon grass skewers with
  lime cheese 236
lemon grass snails 80–1
mussels and clams with
  lemon grass and coconut
  milk 71
northern fish curry 116
pork on lemon grass
  sticks 152
spicy tofu with basil and
  peanuts 93
Thai vegetable curry with
  lemon grass rice 94–5
lemons
  lemon sauce with chicken 132
lettuce
  lettuce leaves and fragrant
    mushrooms 208
  Vietnamese table salad 217
light soy sauce 175
lime 114
  brown rice with lime and
    lemon grass 183
  kaffir lime leaves 85
  pak choi with lime dressing 200
  seared beef salad in a lime
    dressing 169
lobster and crab steamed in
  beer 115
lotus
  lotus stem salad with
    shallots and shredded
    fresh basil 219
low-fat spreads 13
lychees 16

M
mackerel 24, 26
mangoes 16
  green mango salad 213
  mangoes with sticky rice 240–1
marinades 13
meat 23; *see* beef; *see* lamb;
  see pork
  cha shao 155
  lean cuts 12
  meat dishes 151, 152, 155–7,
    159, 162–4, 173–4
  nutrition 26
microwaved foods 13
mint
  fragrant rice with chicken,
    mint and nuoc cham 136
  sweet-and-sour cucumber
    with chillies, coriander and
    mint 218
mirin 63
mixed vegetable soup 36
mooli 14, 15
morning glory with garlic and
  shallots 204
mushrooms 15, 22
  fragrant mushrooms in lettuce
    leaves 208
  hot and sour soup 53
  tofu soup with mushrooms
    and tomato 35

mussels
  mussels and clams with lemon
    grass and coconut milk 71
  pan-steamed mussels with
    lemon grass, chilli and Thai
    herbs 70
  steamed mussels with chilli
    and ginger 111

N
noodles 8, 18
  aromatic broth with roast
    duck, pak choi and egg
    noodles 50
  beef noodle soup 54–5
  cellophane noodle soup 31
  egg noodles 66
  mixed meat noodles 194–5
  noodles and vegetables in
    coconut sauce 188
  plain noodles with four
    flavours 186
  rice noodles with fresh
    herbs 190
  rice noodles with pork 197
  steamboat 191
  stir-fried noodles in seafood
    sauce 193
  sweet and hot vegetable
    noodles 189
  Thai noodles with Chinese
    chives 187
  wheat noodles with stir-fried
    pork 196
northern fish curry 116
northern prawn and squash
  soup 42
nuoc cham 136
nutrition chart 26–7
nuts 16
  nutrition 27

O
oils 13
  nutrition 27
omelette soup 32
orange sauce 147
oyster mushrooms 207
oyster sauce
  stir-fried beef in oyster
    sauce 173

P
pak choi 14
  aromatic broth with roast
    duck, pak choi and egg
    noodles 50–1
  pak choi with lime
    dressing 200
palm sugar 243
pan-steamed mussels with
  lemon grass, chilli and
  Thai herbs 70
pancakes 18–19
  Nonya spring roll
    pancakes 18
  popiah 74–5
  reheating 18

papayas
  green papaya salad 212
  papaya sauce 238–9
  papayas in jasmine flower
    syrup 234
party foods 57–9, 62, 63,
  65–7, 77–9
pastes
  curry pastes 107
  magic paste 36
peanuts
  chicken satay with peanut
    sauce 130
  spicy tofu with basil and
    peanuts 93
peas
  potato, shallot and garlic
    samosas with green
    peas 58
peppers
  stuffed sweet peppers 84
phoenix prawns *see* fantail
  prawns
pineapple
  duck with pineapple and
    ginger 149
  grilled pineapple with papaya
    sauce 238–9
  pineapple with ginger and
    chilli 206
  pork and pineapple coconut
    curry 162
  sambal nanas 226
  stir-fried pineapple with
    ginger 205
piquant prawn laksa 38
plain noodles with four
  flavours 186
poaching 13
pomelo salad 222
popiah 74–5
pork 23
  baked cinnamon meat
    loaf 166–7
  braised black pepper
    pork 161
  broth with stuffed cabbage
    leaves 37
  cha shao 155
  curried pork with pickled
    garlic 164
  dry-cooked pork strips 154
  hot and sour soup 53

lemon grass pork 159
mixed meat noodles 194–5
pork and pineapple coconut
curry 162
pork and prawn soup with
rice sticks 41
pork on lemon grass
sticks 152
rice noodles with pork 197
rice rolls stuffed with
pork 158
saeng wa of grilled
pork 160
steamboat 191
stir-fried pork and butternut
curry 165
stir-fried pork with dried
shrimp 157
sweet and sour pork
stir-fry 156
sweet and sour pork, Thai
style 163
wheat noodles with stir-fried
pork 196
potatoes
potato, shallot and garlic
samosas with green
peas 58
poultry; see chicken; see duck;
see guinea fowl
poultry dishes 129, 131–4,
138–42, 144–6, 149
prawns 25; see also shrimp
broth with stuffed cabbage
leaves 37
Chinese-style scallops and
prawns 110
firecrackers 66
green prawn curry 106
grilled prawns with lemon
grass 73
hot-and-sour prawn
soup 46–7
jasmine rice with prawns and
Thai basil 184
mixed meat noodles 194–5
northern prawn and squash
soup 42
piquant prawn laksa 38
pork and prawn soup with
rice sticks 41
prawn and cauliflower
curry 114
prawns with yellow curry
paste 107
sambal goreng with
prawns 104
seafood salad with fragrant
herbs 223
sinigang 102
stir-fried long beans with
prawns, galangal and
garlic 105
stir-fried prawns with
tamarind 103
Thai prawn salad with garlic
dressing and frizzled
shallots 224–5

preparation
chicken 140
mushrooms 22
prawns 224
spring rolls 19
tamarind 72
turmeric 145
pumpkin
glazed pumpkin in coconut
milk 87
pumpkin and coconut soup 40
pumpkin pudding in banana
leaves 244
stewed pumpkin in coconut
cream 240–1

R
red chicken curry with bamboo
shoots 138–9
rice 18
baked rice pudding, Thai-style
247
brown rice with lime and
lemon grass 183
Cambodian bamboo, fish and
rice soup 45
chicken and basil coconut
rice 143
chicken rice soup with lemon
grass 48–9
coconut rice 178
festive rice 182
fragrant rice with chicken,
mint and nuoc cham 136
fried rice with beef 175
garlic and ginger rice with
coriander 180
Indonesian coconut rice 179
jasmine rice with prawns and
Thai basil 184
mangoes with sticky rice
240–1
pork pâté in a banana leaf 61
rice noodles with pork 197
rice rolls stuffed with pork 158
Saigon southern-spiced chilli
rice 181
Singapore rice vermicelli 192
Thai fried rice 185
Thai vegetable curry with
lemon grass rice 94–5
rice vinegar 17

S
saeng wa of grilled pork 160
salads
aubergine salad 220
cabbage salad 221
green papaya salad 212
larp of Chiang Mai 170–1
pomelo salad 222
saeng wa of grilled pork 160
seafood salad with fragrant
herbs 223
sweet and sour salad 214
Thai beef salad 170–1
Thai fruit and vegetable
salad 215
Thai prawn salad with garlic
dressing and frizzled
shallots 224–5
salmon 24, 25
salt and pepper
prawns 69
sambals
sambal goreng with
prawns 104
sambal nanas 226
samosas 59
potato, shallot and garlic
samosas with green
peas 58
sardines 12
sauces
chicken satay with peanut
sauce 130
chicken with lemon sauce 132
fried vegetables with nam
prik 209
grilled pineapple with papaya
sauce 238–9
noodles and vegetables in
coconut sauce 188
pork pâté in a banana
leaf 61
soy 17
steamed fish with chilli
sauce 119
stir-fried beef in oyster
sauce 173
stir-fried noodles in seafood
sauce 193
Thai tempeh cakes with
sweet chilli 63
trout with tamarind and chilli
sauce 125
scallions see spring onions
scallops 25
Chinese-style scallops and
prawns 110
sea bass 25
seafood see also shellfish
coconut and seafood
soup 39
curried seafood with coconut
milk 108–9
stir-fried noodles in seafood
sauce 193
seaweed 15
seeds
nutrition 27

shallots
hot Thai pickled shallots 211
lotus stem salad with shallots
and shredded fresh
basil 219
morning glory with garlic and
shallots 204
northern fish curry 116
potato, shallot and garlic
samosas with green
peas 58

Thai prawn salad with garlic
dressing and frizzled
shallots 224–5
shellfish; see also seafood;
see prawns
Chinese-style scallops and
prawns 110
curried seafood with coconut
milk 108–9
green prawn curry 106
mussels and clams with
lemon grass and coconut
milk 71
nutrition 26
pan-steamed mussels with
lemon grass, chilli and
Thai herbs 70
prawns with yellow curry
paste 107
salt and pepper prawns 69
sambal goreng with
prawns 104
sinigang 102
stir-fried baby squid with
ginger, garlic and
lemon 112
stir-fried prawns with
tamarind 103
shrimp; see also prawns
stir-fried pork with dried
shrimp 157
side dishes 183, 192, 199–201,
203–5, 207–9, 211, 226
Singapore rice vermicelli 192
sinigang 102
snacks 57–9, 62–3, 65–7, 77–9
snails
lemon grass snails 80–1
snake beans
snake beans with tofu 89

soft-shell crabs with chilli
    and salt 68
soups 29
    asparagus and crab soup 33
    cellophane noodle soup 31
    coconut and seafood
        soup 39
    crispy wonton soup 52
    ginger, chicken and coconut
        soup 46–7
    hot and sour prawn
        soup 46–7
    hot and sour soup 53
    hot and sweet vegetable
        and tofu soup 34
    mixed vegetable soup 36
    northern prawn and squash
        soup 42
    omelette soup 32
    piquant prawn laksa 38
    pumpkin and coconut
        soup 40
    spicy green bean soup 30
    squash and prawn soup 42
    Thai fish broth 44
southern chicken curry 140
southern-style yam 207
soy sauce 175
soya milk
    soya beansprout herb
        salad 216
spices 73
    baked cinnamon meat
        loaf 166–7
    pork pâté in a banana leaf 61
    steamed vegetables with
        Chiang Mai spicy dip 203
spicy green bean soup 30
spicy pan-seared tuna with
    cucumber, garlic and
    ginger 122
spicy tofu with basil and
    peanuts 93
spring onions 15
spring rolls
    cha gio and nuoc cham 67
    crispy Shanghai spring
        rolls 77
    Nonya spring roll pancakes 18
    spring rolls with mushrooms
        and pork 72
    Thai spring rolls 78–9
    tung tong 62

squash and prawn soup 42
squashes
    stir-fried pork and butternut
        curry 165
squid 25
    griddled squid and tomatoes
        in a tamarind dressing 113
    stir-fried baby squid with
        ginger, garlic and lemon 112
star anise
    beef stew with star anise 172
    coconut jelly with star anise
        fruits 236
star fruit 16
steamboat 191
steaming 8, 13, 27
    morning glory with garlic
        and shallots 204
    steamed custard in
        nectarines 243
    steamed fish with chilli
        sauce 119
    steamed vegetables with
        Chiang Mai spicy dip 203
stewed pumpkin in coconut
    cream 240–1
stir-frying 8–9, 13
    chicken with chillies and
        lemon grass 135
    stir-fried asparagus with
        chilli, galangal and lemon
        grass 202
    stir-fried baby squid
        with ginger, garlic and
        lemon 112
    stir-fried beef in oyster
        sauce 173
    stir-fried chicken with basil
        and chilli 134
    stir-fried long beans with
        prawns, galangal and
        garlic 105
    stir-fried noodles in seafood
        sauce 193
    stir-fried pineapple with
        ginger 205
    stir-fried pork with dried
        shrimp 157
    stir-fried prawns with
        tamarind 103
    wheat noodles with stir-fried
        pork 196
storage
    mushrooms 22
stuffed sweet peppers 84
sweet and hot vegetable
    noodles 189
sweet and sour pork
    stir-fry 156
sweet and sour pork,
    Thai style 163
sweet and sour salad 214
sweet and sour vegetables
    with tofu 92
sweet potatoes
    aubergine and sweet
        potato stew with coconut
        milk 98–9

T
tamarind
    griddled squid and tomatoes
        in a tamarind dressing 113
    stir-fried prawns with
        tamarind 103
    trout with tamarind and chilli
        sauce 125
tapioca
    tapioca pudding 245
    tapioca with banana and
        coconut 246
tempeh
    Thai tempeh cakes with
        sweet chilli 63
Thai asparagus 201
Thai beef salad 170–1
Thai fish broth 44
Thai fragrant rice 126, 182
Thai fried rice 185
Thai fruit and vegetable
    salad 215
Thai marinated sea trout 127
Thai noodles with Chinese
    chives 187
Thai prawn salad with garlic
    dressing and frizzled
    shallots 224–5
Thai spring rolls 78–9
Thai tempeh cakes with sweet
    chilli 63
Thai vegetable curry with
    lemon grass rice 94–5
Thai-style baked rice
    pudding 247

Thai-style trout 126
tofu 23
    hot and sweet vegetable
        and tofu soup 34
    nutrition 27
    snake beans with
        tofu 89
    spicy tofu with basil and
        peanuts 93
    sweet and sour vegetables
        with tofu 92
    tofu and green bean red
        curry 88
    tofu and vegetable Thai
        curry 90–1
    tofu soup with mushrooms
        and tomato 35

tomatoes
    griddled squid and
        tomatoes in a tamarind
        dressing 113
tropical fruit gratin 238–9
trout
    hot and fragrant trout 124
    Thai marinated sea trout 127
    Thai-style trout 126
    trout with tamarind and chilli
        sauce 125
tuna 25
    spicy pan-seared tuna with
        cucumber, garlic and
        ginger 122
tung tong 62
turmeric 145

V
vegetables 14–15, 83
    aubergine and sweet potato
        stew with coconut milk 98–9
    cooking 13
    corn and cashew nut curry 85
    crunchy summer rolls 76
    fried vegetables with nam
        prik 209
    hot and sweet vegetable and
        tofu soup 34
    jungle curry 97
    mixed vegetable soup 36
    noodles and vegetables in
        coconut sauce 188
    nutrition 27
    pickled vegetables 210
    snake beans with tofu 89
    spicy green bean soup 30
    steamed vegetables with
        Chiang Mai spicy dip 203
    stuffed sweet peppers 84
    sweet and hot vegetable
        noodles 189
    sweet and sour vegetables
        with tofu 92
    Thai fruit and vegetable
        salad 215
    Thai vegetable curry with
        lemon grass rice 94–5
    tofu and green bean red
        curry 88
    tofu and vegetable Thai
        curry 90–1
    vegetable forest curry 96
    Vietnamese table salad 217

W
water chestnuts 15
watermelon ice 232
woks 8–9, 13
wontons
    crispy wonton soup 52
    green curry puffs 65
    wrappers 8, 18–19

Y
yams
    southern-style yam 207
yellow chicken curry 145